D0054211

Home Before Dark

ALSO BY
SUSAN CHEEVER

Looking for Work
A Handsome Man
The Cage

Home
Before Dark

✿ ✿ ✿ ✿

Susan Cheever

Houghton Mifflin Company / Boston

Copyright © 1984 by Susan Cheever

All rights reserved. No part of this work may be reproduced
or transmitted in any form or by any means, electronic or
mechanical, including photocopying and recording, or by any
information storage or retrieval system, except as may be
expressly permitted by the 1976 Copyright Act or in writing
from the publisher. Requests for permission should be
addressed in writing to Houghton Mifflin Company,
2 Park Street, Boston, Massachusetts 02108.

Library of Congress Cataloging in Publication Data

Cheever, Susan.
Home before dark.
1. Cheever, John—Biography.   2. Novelists, American—
20th century—Biography.   I. Title.
PS3505.H6428Z59   1984   813'.52   [B]   84-9057
ISBN 0-395-35297-5

Printed in the United States of America

V 10 9 8 7 6 5 4 3 2

A portion of this book has been published, in slightly
different form, in *Esquire*.
Excerpts from John Cheever's journals and letters
copyright © 1983 by Mary W. Cheever, all rights reserved.
Used by permission of Mary W. Cheever.
The author is grateful for permission to reprint
eight lines from "my father moved through dooms of love"
by E. E. Cummings, *Complete Poems 1913–1962*.
Copyright 1940 by E. E. Cummings;
renewed 1968 by Marion Morehouse Cummings.
Reprinted by permission of Harcourt Brace Jovanovich, Inc.

For my brothers,
Benjamin and Federico,
and for Sarah

Acknowledgments

A GREAT MANY PEOPLE have been extraordinarily generous in helping me write this book, in sharing letters and papers, in spending time talking about my father and remembering him, in reading the many drafts of the manuscript, and in giving me support and encouragement to continue with a project that sometimes seemed impossible.

My mother helped me from the beginning with her memories, her letters from my father, her willingness to talk about her husband and their marriage, and most of all by giving her permission to read and use my father's journals. My brothers, Ben and Fred, spent hours with me remembering our father, speculating on his motives, and comparing notes on stories he told about our family. Fred wrote a ten-page letter about his experiences and feelings that was invaluable.

My cousin Jane Cheever Carr also shared her memories and perceptions of my father and his brother, and even spent a day with me tracking down the whereabouts of my father's childhood in the tangle of freeways and gas stations that has grown on the meadows and marshlands where he grew up. I want to thank Jane's brother, my cousin David Cheever, and my more distant cousins, Roger Cheever and his father David Cheever, for providing me with their Cheever genealogy and some crucial insights into my father's family stories.

I want to thank William Maxwell, who provided me with my father's wonderful letters to him over a period of more than forty years, and who spent an afternoon with me talking about *The New Yorker,* as well as Milton Greenstein and Edith Agar at *The New Yorker,* who gave me invaluable help. David Swope, Ann Schoales Thom, Simon Michael Bessie, E. J. Kahn, Jr., Lt. Col. Dennis Coates, Max Zimmer, Hope Lange, John Dodds, Janet Malcolm, Ken Burrows, Curt Harnack at Yaddo, John Weaver, George McGrath and the administration of Sing Sing Prison, and the Rev. George Kandel all helped by sharing information or reactions to the manuscript, or both. Patricia Gross did much of the research on my father's early life, scouring school and government records and unearthing essential facts. David B. Green checked the book for accuracy, Susan Colgan hunted down the photographs, and Nan A. Talese at Houghton Mifflin was a supportive and understanding editor.

The Newberry Library in Chicago provided me with Malcolm Cowley's correspondence with my father. The Brandeis University Library made available material from their collection. The staff and administration of Thayer Academy went out of their way to help with transcripts and in locating my father's old classmates. The John Simon Guggenheim Foundation provided me with kindness, encouragement, and financial support in the form of a fellowship. To these and the dozens of others who helped and encouraged me, my thanks.

Preface

WHEN I WAS YOUNG, and my father could see that something was bothering me, he used to suggest that I might try saying a prayer. A prayer for strength, or a prayer for courage. Later, when I began making a living as a journalist, he often suggested that if something disturbed me, I might try writing about it. Keeping a journal helped him a great deal, he said. Putting experience down on paper made it seem less chaotic, less depressing, more sympathetic. "I write to make sense of my life," he used to say.

So in the autumn of 1981, when we found out that my father was going to die soon, it seemed natural that I should write about this. I did, and it helped. I wrote about my feelings, and I wrote about the progress of his illness, and I wrote about cancer in general, and I described trips to hospitals and interviews with doctors, and casual late-night conversations with doctors when they relaxed and confided the truth, and encouraging moments and sad times, and things my father said that seemed important. As the months passed, I found myself writing less and less about the present and more and more about the past. Everything that happened seemed to release a flood of memories of our life together, and of our life as a family, and of the hundreds of stories he had told me about himself and his past and his life as a writer.

In June when my father died, I put away the pile of pages I had written, most of them too painful and too maudlin to reread. I tried going back to the novel I had abandoned in the fall, but I still had a lot to say about my father. So I kept writing, almost in spite of myself. I had always been proud of my independence from my father, and I never intended to become his biographer. Nevertheless, I found my memories and his stories taking a rough narrative shape, and that was how I began to write this book.

At first I thought it would be a slim volume of anecdote and remembrance. I wanted to keep my father alive. I wanted to tell the story of a man who fought to adhere to some transcendent moral standard until the end of his life. I wanted to tell a writer's story. But each memory had layers of reality and fantasy, and unraveling them became a way of discovering who my father really was. I don't think I would have started this book if I had known where it was going to end, but having written it I know my father better than I ever did while he was alive.

Home Before Dark

One

MY FATHER WAS ALWAYS a storyteller. His home-room teacher at Thayer Academy used to promise her class that John would tell a story if they behaved. With luck, and increasing skill, he could spin the story out over two or three class periods so that the teacher and his classmates forgot all about arithmetic and geography and social studies. He told them stories about ship captains and eccentric old ladies and orphan boys, gallant men and dazzling women in a world where the potent forces of evil and darkness were confounded and good triumphed in the end. He peopled his tales with his own family and friends and neighbors from the surrounding Massachusetts South Shore towns: Quincy, Hingham, Hanover, Braintree, Norwell, and Wollaston, where he lived in a big clapboard house on the Winthrop Avenue hill with his mother, an Englishwoman whose family had immigrated to Boston when she was six, his father, a gentleman sailor who owned a prosperous shoe factory in nearby Lynn, and his older brother, Fred, who was going away to Dartmouth in the fall.

My father told these stories over and over again all his life. He wrote them into short stories and novels, and he passed them on to his children. He won the National Book Award, and the Howells Medal from the American Academy of Arts and Letters, and the Pulitzer Prize, and the National Book Critics Circle Award, and the National Medal for Literature. He also kept us amused. Still, he never got the stories quite right. Otherwise, how can you explain the way he kept changing them, embroidering some anecdotes and shifting the emphasis in others, adding sequences and even characters, as if he was searching for some ideal balance that might set him free?

As he grew older, my father became increasingly reluctant to talk about his early years, especially to psychiatrists, who invariably zeroed in on his anger at his dominating mother and his identification with his weak father. Later, when he became famous and journalists' questions forced him to talk about his childhood, he patched together a background of suggestions and half-truths that implied a happy youth and a slow but steady progress in his chosen career. It wasn't so.

"It seems that in my coming of age I missed a year — perhaps a day or an hour," he wrote in his journal twenty years after he left home. "The consecutiveness of growth has been damaged. But how can I go back and find this moment that was lost?"

The critical moment was almost certainly lost in the mid-1920s, when my father was an adolescent and the Cheever family's comfortable way of life began to disintegrate. His father had sold his interest in the shoe factory, Whitteridge and Cheever, and invested the profits in stocks that dwindled in value during the late 1920s and became worthless after the stock-market crash of 1929. By 1926, my grandmother had opened a little gift shop on Granite Street in Quincy to help support the family, but in the fall of 1928 money was so short that my grandparents could no longer pay tuitions, and my father dropped out of Thayer Academy and enrolled in Quincy High School; his grades slid from gentlemen's C's and C minuses to D's and E's. When he returned to Thayer in 1929 to repeat his junior year, his mother was paying the school bills. Fred left Dartmouth and came home to look for a job. When he arrived, still redolent with the glamour of campus life, he met and co-opted my father's girlfriend, Iris Gladwin.

My grandfather, once a dapper, literate businessman who read Shakespeare to his sons, became desperate and bitterly sorry for himself. In 1930 he was forced to begin borrowing from the Wollaston Cooperative Bank against the fine house at 123 Winthrop Avenue. (In 1933 the bank repossessed the house and tore it down.) The family's financial disaster became a personal disaster. My father's parents were separated, and although they were later reconciled, no one in the family was ever reconciled to their new circumstances. His mother expanded her business to a larger gift shop on Hancock Street and began running a tearoom during the summers. Being supported by his wife was a humiliating experience for my grandfather. At home there were angry fights and terrible silences. My father's parents, locked in their private agonies, hardly seemed to notice him. Had they ever noticed him? The unhappiness of those years cast deep shadows over the past as well as the future.

His parents' separation was symbolized for him by "an afternoon when he returned home from school and found the furnace dead, some unwashed dishes on the table in the dining room and at the center of the table a pot of tulips that the cold had killed and blackened," he wrote in his journal in the 1950s, expressing his feelings through a third-person narrator, as he often did. "The realization that anger had driven them both out of the house, that their passionate detestation of one another had blinded them to their commitments to the house and to him traveled crookedly up through his heart like a fissure made by an earthquake in a wall, leaving on one side innocence and trust and on the other the lingering ruefulness and gloom of an orphaned spirit. He never quite escaped the chill of that empty house, and all the symbols of exile — the lighted window on the distant farm, the watch dog's barking, the ship going out to sea, the bright voices of children playing in the distance — held for him so unnatural a force that they could make it seem as if his heart had turned over."

My father's story, as he usually told it, begins with his final departure from Thayer Academy in March of 1930, his junior year, and his flight to New York City. There his first short story, "Expelled," was published by *The New Republic* in October 1930, when he was eighteen. Typically, there are many different versions of these events.

"It didn't come all at once," the story in *The New Republic* begins. "It took a very long time. First I had a skirmish with the English department and then all the other departments. Pretty soon something had to be done."

In the story, a boy filled with lively curiosity, quick intelligence, and the love of nature clashes with a school where knowledge is less important than college admissions and curiosity is not allowed. The boy is expelled. He is right, but he is all alone. Autumn comes.

"Everyone is preparing to go back to school," the story explains. "I have no school to go back to.

"I am not sorry. I am not at all glad."

Sometimes my father would say that he had been kicked

out of Thayer for smoking. Sometimes he suggested that his attitude as a student had left something to be desired. He once let drop that he had taught himself German in order to show up a mediocre teacher's interpretation of Goethe. Once or twice he told me that *he* didn't like the quality of the teachers and administrators at Thayer. He had won a scholarship to Harvard, he said, but when his name was read out in morning chapel on a list of students being considered for suspension, he had walked out of the chapel and the school forever.

The Cheevers are very good at walking out. "When I remember my family, I always remember their backs," he wrote in his journal. "They were always indignantly leaving places . . . They were always stamping out of concerts, sports events, theatres. If Koussevitzky thinks I'll sit through that! That umpire is a crook. This play is filthy. I didn't like the way that waiter looked at me. They saw almost nothing to its completion, and that's the way I remember them, heading for an exit."

At other times, my father would say he left Thayer after the bank foreclosed on the Wollaston house and his family moved temporarily to Aunt Mary Thompson's farmhouse in Hanover — although in fact this did not happen until a few years later. The world seemed to have gone awry. His father was drinking heavily and had begun the debilitating rounds of unsuccessful job interviews that would go on the rest of his life. At times his losses seemed to be driving him crazy. My father's own aunt Anna Boynton Thompson, once a respected classics scholar, was starving herself to death in the upper rooms of her house in Braintree. It was her protest against Abdul-Hamid II's massacre of the Armenians. And his mother was running a gift shop.

Mary Liley Cheever had always been a cheery "make-do"

sort of woman, with tiny deft hands and a passionate dedication to Mrs. Mary Baker Eddy's Christian Science. But she also had her dark side: claustrophobia, impatience, a stubborn desire to control. She insisted on self-reliance, and although she had been a nurse before she married, she did not believe in medicine. (My father had a childhood bout with tuberculosis that wasn't even diagnosed until his lungs were X-rayed and showed the scar tissue years later.) When she broke her leg in a fall in the bathtub when she was a middle-aged widow, she refused medical care and let the bone heal itself. A broken leg can be excruciatingly painful, but she did not want medication. She limped for the rest of her life.

"And thinking of mother, while I shave, it seems to me that she lived her life by a set of values that I never understood: fire, water, loneliness and prayer," my father wrote soon after she died in 1953. "Many things that were close to the earth: the smell of new bread, lilacs, earth; the sound of running water. It seemed to me at times I was not meant to understand this set of values; that they were intentionally arcane; that their strength was in their complexity."

But one thing that his mother told him, my father understood too well. They had not wanted another child before he was born. His conception was a drunken accident between two people who no longer cared about each other. When his mother found out that she was pregnant, his father had tried to force her to have an abortion.

❅ ❅ ❅

After my grandfather had lost the shoe factory and his life savings, it might have seemed a natural thing for his wife to open a little shop. My grandmother had a genteel English manner that made her the perfect teashop hostess. It might have seemed natural, that is, to anyone except my grandfather. To him, his wife's competence was an emasculation, a perversion of the Yankee male ethic that had been his mainstay and his anchor. My father observed and remembered, in Wollaston, in Hanover, and later when he came home to visit Quincy, where my grandparents had settled and my grandmother had established a new, larger Mary L. Cheever Gift Shop.

She hooked rugs and painted lampshades and filled bottles with seashells and covered bricks with printed fabric to make doorstops, and she struck bargains on tea sets and hand-crocheted antimacassars. All his life my father hated any objects or furnishings that suggested the bibelots and toilet-water-scented atmosphere of a gift shop. Inlaid boxes, agate eggs, china dogs and cats, curtains with valances, doilies, and guest towels all gave him an intense, nauseating claustrophobia. They seemed to threaten the true, delightful, innocent order of the world. They seemed to pollute the clear air and darken the blue skies and muddle the sexes. In my father's first novel, *The Wapshot Chronicle*, the Wapshot brothers' mother Sarah turns their father's beloved boat, the *Topaze*, into New England's Only Floating Gift Shoppe. An earlier story, "Publick House," is an account of a young man returning to visit his childhood home, which has been turned into a tearoom by his mother. The family heirlooms are being sold off to tourists who would prefer reproductions, his mother is too busy with the paying guests to pay any attention to him, and the grandfather in the story is a wasted old man who lives upstairs, above the chattering ladies, like a ghost of the past.

Another time, my father told me that his plan had been to leave Thayer and set up housekeeping in nearby Boxford with his older brother Fred. After their parents' separation the two brothers had become very close, and in 1931 they went off together on a low-budget walking tour through Germany and Great Britain. Fred had apparently been forgiven for taking away Iris. He also had a job, and he would soon go to work for Pepperell Manufacturing Company. In the Cheever family, Fred already represented the forces of stability and probity. My father was to be the artist. Two oil portraits painted by their mother's sister, Florence Liley Young, show Fred looking ruddy and substantial in a business suit, and John, who was seven years younger, with tousled locks and wearing a blue painter's smock. Their parents' failure had encouraged the two brothers to depend on each other, and it was arranged that Fred would support them while my father established himself as a writer in New York and Boston. They adored one another, and in the Boston community, at least, it wasn't unusual for two bachelor brothers to live together for a while, or forever.

But love was already a complicated business for my father. His love for his older brother, who nurtured and supported him — and whom he was later called on to nurture and support — was certainly the most powerful and complicated attachment in his life. It was so powerful that he had to get away from it. "It was the strongest love in my life," he told me once. "When it became apparent that it was an ungainly closeness, I packed my bag and shook his hand and left." Ungainly closeness was to be avoided absolutely. Instead of renting the house in Boxford and moving in with his beloved brother as they had planned, my father left the South Shore and went to seek his fortune in New York City. After he left, Fred married Iris.

In all the different stories about my father dropping out of Thayer and leaving home, he always arrived in the city in the autumn of 1930, a few months after his eighteenth birthday. While he was trying to get a start in New York, his parents lost the Wollaston house and spent three years staying with friends and family or in summer rentals before they eventually settled in Quincy. His mother ran the gift shop. His father looked for a job. After my grandfather died in 1946, my father found in his desk copies of more than fifty job applications he had sent off with no success, as well as letters to Jim Farley, Jim Curley, and the King of England, and a long correspondence with the Massachusetts Registry of Motor Vehicles about losing his four-digit license plate to an Italian politician. Fred and Iris moved to Norwell, built an authentic Swiss chalet in a grove of pines, and started raising their family, although Fred's Pepperell salary was still being used to subsidize his parents and my father in New York. My father often went to Norwell or Quincy for long visits, and he spent the summer with his parents when New York got too hot and too expensive. But the South Shore was never his home again — if it ever had been.

"He would remember with pleasure as the most beautiful part of the world the roads south of Hingham with their pollarded elms and the smell there of timothy and sweet grass in the hay and the salt marshes on the North River and the river itself with its strong smelling waters and even the peaceful hill at Adams as quiet as a country village with its elms and its distant church bells," he wrote after his father's funeral in Norwell. There had been a scene at the graveside. There were always scenes. His mother insisted that his father had wanted Prospero's speech from *The Tempest* — "Our revels now are ended . . ." — recited over his grave. My father refused to do it.

"But beyond the country skies, beneath the peace of the

Hingham lanes, deeper than memory but acting with the force of a remembered crime, was something that would always lead him away and not only away but far away so that when he stepped from Grand Central into the traffic of 42nd Street and only then did he feel that he was free. They had been poor there. That was one thing. They had been unhappy there."

About fifty years after my father left the South Shore for New York City, after he had gone through poverty and success and alcoholism and collapse and success again and celebrity to become finally established and prosperous, I too began to make a living writing fiction. My father seemed to be pleased when my first novel was published, and my second. But I think he also feared for me; he wanted me to have a more secure and happier life than he had had. He was always more of a father than a colleague. We used to have a friendly competition about who could find or invent the best titles. When one of us came up with a good one, we would argue about who would get to use it. I don't know where he found the last one he came up with, in the summer of 1980, but it had a special resonance for both of us. It was *Home Before Dark.*

"Oh, I'm going to use that one!" I said.

"Oh no you're not," he said. "It's mine." But we both found other names for the books we were working on.

Home before dark. My father liked to tell a story about my younger brother Fred. When Fred was a little boy, we lived in a small house on a big estate called Beechwood, in Scarborough, New York, about twenty-five miles up the Hudson River from New York City. Once, at twilight after a long summer day, my father was standing outside the house under the big elm tree that shaded the flagstones in front of the door. Fred came back from playing with some friends, worn out and tired too, and when he saw Daddy standing there he ran across the grass and threw his little boy's body into his father's arms.

"I want to go home, Daddy," he said, "I want to go home." Of course he *was* home, just a few feet from the front door, in fact. But that didn't make any difference, as my father well understood. We all want to go home, he would say when he told this story. We all do.

Two

AND THINKING HOW our origins catch up with us I wonder what I will have to pay on this account," my father wrote in his journal in 1961. "I have been a storyteller since the beginning of my life, rearranging facts in order to make them more interesting and sometimes more significant. I have turned my eccentric old mother into a woman of wealth and position and made my father a captain at sea. I have improvised a background for myself — genteel, traditional — and it is generally accepted. But what are the bare facts, if I were to write them. The yellow house, the small north living room with a player piano and on a card table a small stage where I made scenery and manipulated puppets. The old mahogany gramophone with its crank, its pitiful power of reproduction. In the dining room an overhead lamp made from the panels of a mandarin coat. Against the wall the helm of my father's sailboat — long gone, inlaid with mother of pearl."

My father always told us that the first member of our family to emigrate from England to the new world was

Ezekiel Cheever, who arrived in Boston Harbor on the *Arbella* in 1630. The *Arbella* was the trim flagship of the privately financed "Winthrop fleet," eleven ships carrying more than a hundred families who hoped to settle on the rocky coast of New England and establish a community where they could live and worship without interference from the king or anyone else. She was a ship of wise men: the clergy, teachers, and leaders who had waited to be sure there was a need for them before entrusting their valuable souls to the treacherous North Atlantic. The roughnecks had come on the *Mayflower*. The Reverend George Phillips was on the *Arbella*, and John Winthrop, who was to be the first governor of the Massachusetts Bay Colony.

Ezekiel Cheever was in his early twenties when he arrived in Boston. After teaching Latin for a while in New Haven and in Ipswich, Massachusetts, he finally became the master of the renowned Boston Latin School. His primer *Accidence, a Short Introduction to the Latin Tongue* is still referred to, and by the time he died in 1708, he was so well respected that his student Cotton Mather delivered the eulogy at his funeral. "A rare incidence of Piety, Strength, Health and Ableness," wrote Judge Samuel Sewall, another eminent Bostonian, who visited Ezekiel every day during the week he died. "The Welfare of the Province was much upon his spirit. He abominated periwigs." My father loved to quote the part about abominating periwigs.

I have two younger brothers. The older one, Benjamin Hale, who was born in 1948 when I was five years old, is named after our great-great-grandfather, a ship captain in the China trade who sailed out of Newburyport in the 1700s. My mother has special shelves filled with the blue and white Canton china that Benjamin Hale brought back as ballast from the Orient. A Chinese fan of his is framed in the upper hallway of my parents' house in Ossining, and a tiny pair of wire-rimmed spectacles in a lacquered case is kept in my grandmother's sewing box, which sits on a desk in the upstairs library.

My younger brother, Federico, was born in 1957, the year we all lived in Italy. He is called Fred, and he has grown up to be the member of our family who best understands the conglomeration of dates, events, and ideas called history. Fred likes to know the facts, and so when he got to school he looked up the manifest of the ship *Arbella*. Ezekiel Cheever's name wasn't on it. His career in New England was well documented, but there was no record of how he got there.

It turns out that Ezekiel Cheever sailed from London and Southampton on the chartered ship *Hector*, which arrived in Boston in 1637, bound for Connecticut. I found this out in the side gallery of the New York Public Library devoted to genealogy and local history, as I traced the Cheever ancestry through the dusty, crumbling volumes of historical registers and ships' passenger lists and finally the Yale University Press publication *Passengers on the Hector*. What Cheever ancestor of mine, I wonder, changed Ezekiel's story so that he came instead on the *Arbella*? The *Arbella* was a more aristocratic boat, but the *Hector* had her own distinctions. She was carrying the precious library that had been collected in England for the new colony, and Ezekiel's fellow passengers included the Davenports, Theophilus Eaton, who was to become governor of Connecticut, and Thomas Yale, whose family later endowed a little college in New Haven.

At any rate, generations of Cheevers settled and prospered in and around Boston and up the coast as far north (or east, as they would say) as Maine. They were a seafaring family, and although some were bankers and merchants, most were yeomen or joiners, master mariners or merchant seamen, ship's mates or captains. They were a numerous and industrious clan, and by the nineteenth century the Cheevers had become an established Brahmin family concentrated in the picturesque towns of Boston's patrician North Shore.

It was Grandfather Cheever who started all the trouble, my father always told me. Rebellious and atheistic even as a young man, he wrote a letter to Dr. David Cheever — an illustrious Boston physician who was a distant cousin — announcing that he intended to donate his body to medical science for the purpose of anatomical studies after his death. The family was appalled, my father said. It was unthinkable for a Cheever to forgo the Christian burial service. Tolerance was not the hallmark of Boston society, and after that our branch of the Cheevers was summarily severed from the family tree. My father's brother Fred told his children a different story with the same ending. Grandfather Cheever had grown up in Newburyport on the North Shore and shipped out as a merchant seaman, he said. He had a girl in every port, and even in the hard-drinking society of sailors, his liquor consumption quickly became legendary. The family warned him about his behavior. Finally, his reputation was too much for the Cheever image. He was confronted by his elders and banished forever to the socially inferior villages of the South Shore.

As a result of this putative schism, however it happened, those of us who were descended from my grandfather Cheever's outcast line have always been aware of being exiles. In our immediate family, at least, we have enjoyed being exiles quite a lot. When we were growing up, my father used to tell us stories about the "other" Cheevers, the "respectable" Cheevers, who lived strait-laced lives and owned a big house in Cambridge and an even bigger one in Wellesley and sent their children to Milton Academy and Harvard and had their names in the social register. It was one thing to be interested in family history, and quite another to care about superficial things like that. We exiles knew the power of the past, but we also understood the transience of worldly circumstances. They could have their humorless Boston respectability with its piss-pot social rules and regulations and its dumpy Richardsonian architecture.

My father loved the name Ezekiel, though. He used it for our first male black Labrador puppy, a barrel-chested dog who made so much noise that we called him Zeke the Shriek. Zeke ran away, but not before my father had commissioned a larger-than-life bronze of his head, dewlaps and all, which sits on a pedestal at the right side of the upstairs fireplace of the house in Ossining. My father tried to persuade my brother Ben to name his son, the first grandchild, Ezekiel. Ben refused. In my father's novel *Falconer*, published in 1977, the main character is named Ezekiel Farragut, after Ezekiel Cheever and the Farragut Parkway exit off the Saw Mill River Parkway on the drive from Westchester to New York City. Ezekiel Farragut is a homosexual drug addict, in jail for the murder of his brother. My father used to tell us that after the book was published, the respectable Cheevers took the name Ezekiel right out of their entries in the social register. He was delighted.

The closest I came to the respectable Cheevers while my father was alive was one summer in Cambridge when I was going to Harvard Summer School to make up credits for my degree at Brown University. I was living in a dingy apartment with five other girls. At night, I could hear the grunts and sighs and the loud creak of bedsprings as my roommate made love to her boyfriend. *My* boyfriend had suggested that we use the summer to see other people. I spent the solitary twilight hours walking and bicycling through the residential streets of Cambridge with their spacious frame houses set back behind great old oaks and maples. When I passed what someone had pointed out to me as "the Cheever house," a big, comfortable-looking place on Brattle Street with flower beds and well-tended lawns, I would peer toward the windows where the respectable Cheevers were at home. Sometimes they would be sitting and reading, or moving against the soft lamplight. Sometimes the murmur of their conversation and laughter filtered out through the curtains to where I stood alone in the gathering darkness.

Of course it's not that simple. No doubt respectable Cheevers have flunked out of school, taken to drink, and married the wrong people and divorced them, just as we have. Even old Ezekiel got into some trouble in New Haven for "uncomely gestures and carriage" in church. He smiled during the sermon. Then, to hide his amusement, he lowered his head and stuffed his handkerchief into his mouth. The tribunal that was called to investigate this egregious behavior chose to believe Ezekiel when he said that a dreadful toothache had caused his grimace, his bowed head, and the application of his handkerchief, but soon after that he moved north to Ipswich.

It was about a year after my father died, and twenty years after that summer in Cambridge, that I looked the respectable Cheevers up in the social register, sat down at the telephone one evening, and dialed the number given for David Cheever, Dedham, Mass., Harvard class of '31, Dedham Country and Polo Club — the oldest son of the Dr. David Cheever to whom my grandfather had written his infamous letter announcing his intention to give his body to science. David Cheever could not have been more cordial.

I could hear a clock chiming the hour in the background as we identified ourselves, and from his melodic Yankee gentleman's voice I imagined him sitting by a fireside sipping Hu-Kwa tea from Canton china.

"Of course I've been asked a million times if I was related to John Cheever," he said, laughing. "I think your father was a genius. We bought his books and we read his stories and we thought they were great." But he had never heard anything about a split in the family. He promised to talk with his brother and get back to me. "I want to help in any way I can," he said.

David Cheever is quietly proud of his kinship to Ezekiel Cheever, and of the fact that he comes from a line of Cheever physicians who have served their country since before the Revolutionary War. His son Roger belongs to the sixth straight generation of Cheever men to have graduated from Harvard. David Cheever sent me the ornate "Cheever Pedigree" his father had had drawn up, paying genealogists for this when he had little money for other things. The family tree shows the generations between David and Ezekiel and traces the lineage back to its Norman origins and the French name Chevre ("goat"), and to William the Conqueror, and the Cheever coat of arms: azure, three goats rampant, gules.

"There never was a schism," David Cheever wrote me. "Your father thought we were a bit formal and in his early days preferred not to be interested in family history. Later he changed and was very much interested."

As it happens, my family *is* related to Ezekiel Cheever — very distantly. My father's great-grandfather was Benjamin Hale, and Benjamin Hale's great-great-grandfather, Israel, who was born in Cambridge, Massachusetts, in 1661, was the son of Daniel Cheever of St. Alphage, Canterbury, England, a first cousin of Ezekiel's who immigrated to America in 1640, a few years after Ezekiel did. But the genealogy doesn't matter, really. As I spoke to David Cheever, I began to understand my father's sense of being an exile. Like many of my father's stories, his version of the schism has an inherent truth, outside of the facts. It wasn't a question of respectable Cheevers and outcast Cheevers, or even — as I had often suspected — of rich Cheevers and poor Cheevers. The members of David Cheever's branch of the family regarded their name with a dignity and seriousness absolutely unknown in our family on any subject. For them, the name Ezekiel has an almost sacred ring. We do not have the privilege of this kind of certainty about who we are.

Of course our family has often desperately coveted the respectable qualities we have so often mocked. My father was confused by this ambivalence, and his older brother Fred may have been destroyed by it. Although he never finished Dartmouth, Fred was handsome enough and bright enough to recoup his status — for a while. He began his professional life in the 1930s as a promising, exceptionally intelligent businessman, prosperous enough to help support his parents, send money to his kid brother who was trying to make it as a writer in New York City, and build his own house. In the summers, Fred and Iris and their children and a nanny went to Nantucket. The children joined the Girl Scouts and the 4-H Club and were enrolled at Milton Academy.

Fred's oldest child, Jane, is the only one of my grandfather's seven grandchildren who stayed near Boston. She lives in Hingham, between Norwell and Quincy, in the rambling gray frame house where her husband grew up. He and Jane were childhood sweethearts, and their children are the third generation to be raised in that house. They are about as respectable as anyone could be, and as nice. Great old trees shade the neighborhood where they live. Jane's husband is a banker. The four children are courteous and attractive. Their eyes are blue. They have a sailboat. They go to church. Their lawns are neatly mowed, and there is a statue of Abraham Lincoln at the end of their street.

❊   ❊   ❊

At the beginning of December in 1981, the doctors told us that my father was dying, but none of us could bear to talk about funeral arrangements. It was too soon, it was always too soon. By the time my mother thought to mention it, ten days before he died, my father was too weak to respond. He wouldn't have anyway. When the subject came up in family conversations, he had always suggested that we bury him in the back yard. We knew this was a joke, but what it meant was that he didn't care about things like that. It also meant that he wasn't going to die. Now, without his joking, we didn't know what to do. There was no family to turn to, really; Fred and Iris had both died in 1976. There was no place to bury him where he had lived, and my father had always made it abundantly clear that the Episcopalian church he went to in Ossining was attended out of convenience rather than preference.

It was my mother's idea to call Cousin Jane. She remembered that Fred and my grandfather were buried up there somewhere, and besides, she didn't know who else to ask. Jane took over. It turned out that her parents and our grandparents were buried together in the Norwell Center cemetery. It was a pretty place, Jane said, across a green from a simple white wooden church. The funeral director who had handled the arrangements for our grandparents and her parents would take care of everything. His name was Mr. Wadsworth, at the Sparrell Funeral Home in Norwell.

I called Mr. Wadsworth and gave him the information he

needed, and he told me a little more about the Norwell Center cemetery and the members of our family who were buried there. Life always came full circle, Mr. Wadsworth told me — his father had buried my grandmother. He explained that the graveyard plot in Norwell had been bought decades ago by my grandfather Cheever for his wife and sons. Since my father was the last surviving member of his generation, the plot now belonged to him. I don't know if my father knew about this. He certainly never mentioned it. But it was there all along, a grassy spot under a big maple on the side of a hill a few miles from where he was born.

Three

WHEN HE ARRIVED IN New York City in 1930, my father started making the rounds of editors' offices with his stories and looking for any writing work he could get. Malcolm Cowley, a junior editor at *The New Republic*, bought "Expelled" and published it in the October 10 issue. Eventually *Hound and Horn*, *Collier's*, *Story* magazine, *Harper's Bazaar*, and *The Yale Review* also bought stories. Metro-Goldwyn-Mayer paid him five dollars a book for writing synopses. This was a start, but he still didn't have enough money to live on. Fred sent him ten dollars a week, and my father rented a room in a boarding house at 633 Hudson Street for three dollars a week. When he couldn't afford the rent, he moved out and stayed with friends. Every day he bought a bottle of milk and marked it into five portions to make it last. His typewriter was about all he had except a past he was determined to escape, a future that looked like an even chance, and a couple of friends who thought he could write.

When he got really hungry, he would take the train up

to Boston and move in with his parents or Fred wherever they were staying. At least they fed him, although the atmosphere at home made work almost impossible. "I don't expect to do anything worth publishing for five years or so," he wrote Cowley despairingly from the house on Spear Street in Quincy where his parents had finally settled. "There is a lot of time. I don't even know what I want to do but I have discovered that knowing what you want to do has very little effect on getting the work at hand actually done."

Cowley, an older man who had been an ambulance driver in World War I, became a close friend, and over the years he gave my father a great deal of support and strong editorial advice. It was his suggestion that we live in Europe for a while; he was right in thinking that this would broaden my father's understanding of the world. And in later years he often urged my father to stop writing about the trivialities of suburban life and take on something more important. The photographer Walker Evans was another good friend. Evans took a picture of my father's boarding-house room on Hudson Street that is in the Museum of Modern Art now. My father used to say that Walker took the photograph because he couldn't believe that anyone could live in such a miserable place. His camera captured the mood of summer in a tenement, and the pathetic, saving neatness of the poor. In the photograph, an old-fashioned iron bedstead has a thin, carefully folded quilt in one corner. The sheets are perfectly tucked. The blind in the one window is drawn, and a hot afternoon light gleams from around its edges through sagging muslin curtains.

"The skyline of course was all different, even in the Village," my father remembered years later in another letter to Cowley. "When you went to the window you heard phonographs and radios, a soft sound, never the gunfire from TV and of course there were no antennae, no air conditioners. I have an undated [journal] entry describing a crowd gathered around a 1910 Pierce Arrow parked in front of Rikers. Niles Spencer, fairly drunk, is standing on the running board saying: 'Don't you laugh at this car, don't you dare laugh at this car. The world in 1910 was a much better place than you have ever known.' "

My father's generation in the 1930s were young men and women caught between the memory of one war and the expectation of another. During his trip to Germany with Fred in 1931, my father had seen enough to convince him that another war was more than possible. Years later he wrote Cowley, "Before I left Hanover [Massachusetts] for the last time I spaded the vegetable garden and planted a potato patch. It was Memorial Day. I could hear the band in the village. I thought I would never return to eat the potatoes I had planted (I don't like potatoes) and that in the years ahead the approach of war would trim and color most of my impulses." It was a hard squeeze to grow up with. Some of my father's New York friends drank and tried to forget about it. Others planned to ship out for Honduras or South America. Many were political radicals, and some joined the Communist Party. (In Boston, my father and Fred had gone to meetings of the John Reed club.) They turned against a capitalism that seemed to have failed, threw off the conservatism of their parents, and took on a listless, angry politics of their own.

"Born in the vicinity of 1912, we come as strangers to this wreck," he wrote in 1934 in a sketch called "Letter from the Mountains," which was rejected by the editors at *The New Republic* as "defeatist material." "All we remember of the war is cheering in a hot playground on Armistice;

we knew none of the dead. We wait in homes, in furnished rooms, waiting for trains, for jobs, for girls, for coming of age. One is married. One is jailed for inciting to riot. One is dead. We have refused their drinks, walked away from the old gang and having come this far we stand by the window, rooting for some sweet certainty like a hand in an empty pocketbook."

My father was having a wonderful time, though. All his life he liked to tell stories about his own poverty, and the hardships of being a young writer in New York, and the squalid room on Hudson Street. I think he was proud that he had done it that way and been penniless and unknown at the beginning. He started with nothing but his own experience and pulled his whole life and work out of the rich air of his imagination. In those days it wasn't at all certain that he could make a living as a writer. (*The New Yorker* didn't buy a short story of his until 1935.) His hope was to land a staff job at *The New Republic* or the *New York Times*, with a regular salary. People didn't want to hire a kid with no high school diploma. He experimented with spelling his by-line "Jon," and wrote his letters in lower case like his new acquaintance E. E. Cummings. There were still people like Cummings who called him Joey, as his parents had when he was in short pants. (He had been christened John William, but he quickly dropped his middle name.) New York City women dazzled him, and he was thrilled to make the rounds of the Greenwich Village speakeasies (the Eighteenth Amendment was repealed in 1933) and to meet the city's literary men and women: Cowley, Kenneth Burke, Edmund Wilson, Cummings, Hart Crane, Hazel Hawthorne, Katharine White and Harold Ross at *The New Yorker*, Lincoln Kirstein at *Hound and Horn*. When Malcolm Cowley and his wife Peggy invited my father to his first New

York literary party, he put on his only jacket and went off with great expectations.

"I was offered two kinds of drinks. One was greenish. The other was brown. They were both, I believe, made in a bathtub," he remembered forty years later at a testimonial dinner for Cowley given by the Newberry Library in Chicago. "I was told that one was a Manhattan and the other was Pernod. My only intent was to appear terribly sophisticated and I ordered a Manhattan . . . I went on drinking Manhattans lest anyone think I came from a small town like Quincy, Massachusetts. Presently after four or five Manhattans I realized I was going to vomit. I rushed to Mrs. Cowley, thanked her for the party, and reached the apartment house hallway where I vomited all over the wallpaper. Malcolm never mentioned the damages."

Soon after my father's stories started appearing in *The New Republic,* Cowley introduced him to Mrs. Elizabeth Ames, the director of Yaddo, a recently established writers' colony in Saratoga Springs, New York. Yaddo was a Gothic mansion with a sizable endowment from its late owner Katrina Trask Peabody, the widow of Spencer Trask, a wealthy financier. Mrs. Trask, whose children had died of childhood illnesses, had had a dream that after her death men and women would walk through her woods and over Yaddo's grand terraces "creating . . . creating . . . creating." There were no vacancies at Yaddo when my father first applied to Mrs. Ames in April of 1933. "Other than Malcolm's word and a few published stories I have little to recommend me," he wrote to Mrs. Ames from a temporary apartment on Pinckney Street in Boston. "I am planning to be a writer and have been working for the last year on apprenticeship prose." But in 1934 he went to Yaddo at last.

At first he helped around the place and acted as Mrs.

Ames's assistant to help defray the expenses of his long stays. One summer he had a lovely time running the old Garwood power launch, which took the mail from Bolton Landing on Lake George out to Triuna — a Venetian fantasy of bridges, domes, and archways that the Trasks had built on three small islands. Yaddo became his home, and the genteel Mrs. Ames became his mentor, whether he liked it or not. She loaned him money, made sure he had time to work at writing, and scolded him for not trying harder to get another kind of job — a job that might support him while he learned to write. He replied testily that he had worked all his life and that he was unable to find a job because he had no qualifications, no experience, and no degree. He dredged up anecdotes from his past and wrote dazzling letters to convince Mrs. Ames that he was right in pursuing his career as a writer exclusively. He knew how practical she was; he even worked on his spelling.

"New England was quite an experience," he wrote her after a visit to his parents in Quincy in 1937.

My father's memory is very acute and colorful and his story is very exciting. He remembers the typhoid after the Civil War that laid an already impoverished and disillusioned Newburyport even lower. He remembers his mother's delirium and his Aunt Juliana who used to sit among the mandarin coats and ivory junks that her husband brought back from the east and talk with an Indian "medium." His Uncle Ebenezer was an abolitionist. He ran a biscuit factory that turned out hard tack for the sailing vessels. When the war between the states was declared he was offered a contract by the government to make hard tack for the soldiers. He rejected the offer because he felt his hard tack wasn't good enough for Union soldiers. A competitor named Pierce then accepted the contract and made a fortune and founded a dynasty on the proceeds. Uncle Ebenezer had no regrets. He played the flute. The Pierce bakery has since grown into the National Biscuit Company while the wind whistles through Uncle Ebenezer's abandoned flour mill.

And then my father came up to Boston on the *Harold Currier*, the last sailing vessel to leave the Newburyport Yards. That was the end of an epoch. After that came the Boston fire. At the turn of the century he was shooting off Roman candles on the common with the rest of his generation. He was making a lot of money then. Then came the stories of oyster sweepstakes in Chesapeake Bay, storms on Lake Erie, express trains to Idaho, gold-rushes, horse races, chaffard à la presse and mushrooms under glass, breakfasts in New Orleans, champagne, Shakespeare, boxing matches, old age and failure. New England began its tragic decline. They tore down the Parker House. They closed the mills. And I saw Amoskeag [Mill] last fall, [empty and] looking at its own reflection in the Merrimac.

My father worked on his short stories at Yaddo in the 1930s and 1940s, on his first novel, *The Wapshot Chronicle*, in the 1950s, on *Bullet Park* in the 1960s, on *Falconer* in the 1970s, and on *Oh What a Paradise It Seems* in the 1980s. When he was young he learned from the older writers at Yaddo — Katherine Anne Porter, Cowley, James T. Farrell, who was working on *Studs Lonigan* there that first year, and the novelist Josephine Herbst, who became a close friend of his for the rest of her life. When he was older, he improved his friendships with contemporaries like Saul Bellow and younger writers like Philip Roth, Jules Feiffer, and his own former students Max Zimmer and Allan Gurganus. He was watching the World Series on television at Yaddo in 1980 when he had the first of two grand mal seizures that in retrospect seemed to herald his final illness. When he made money, he donated it to Yaddo, and he was a director and the vice president of the Corporation of Yaddo when he died.

My father was always a conscientious elder statesman,

and Yaddo was just one way in which he provided oppor-
tunities for the writers he admired. He served on dozens of
prize juries and grants committees, and he campaigned very
hard to get other, usually younger, writers into the National
Institute of Arts and Letters and later into the American
Academy. If he felt any rivalry with his colleagues, he made
a point of never acknowledging it. "Fiction is not a competitive sport," he used to say. He said it so often, in fact,
that it became a family joke.

You can see the stone tower of Yaddo from the Northway
after the road passes Albany, but the entrance is an un-
obtrusive driveway down the street from the old-fashioned
wooden sheds at the Saratoga track. The drive winds up
past ponds and through dark groves of pines and hemlocks
to the gigantic façade of the main house. The Trasks built it
as a full-dress country seat with interior fountains, servants'
quarters, elaborate outbuildings, including a family chapel,
and a music room that holds two hundred people. An entire
German community was transplanted to Saratoga to do the
panelings and the *boiserie* that surround the long leaded
windows and the acres of Tiffany stained glass. It's a real
castle: my father told us that Mrs. Trask sent cables to
Queen Victoria signed "To the Queen of England from the
Queen of Yaddo." But the Trasks were definitely New
World. The name Yaddo came from one of their children's
lisped descriptions of a shadow thrown by the pine trees
onto one of the many ornamental ponds. Tiffany was commissioned to do a wall-sized glass window, at the landing
of the great staircase, of a woman in a long gown holding a
single flower. My father always said the woman was Katrina
Trask.

"The noise of the carpet sweeper woke me this morning,
the country house touch," he wrote my mother in 1939, the

year after they met. "That and an ant wandering over what they used to call Turkey carpets. It's after breakfast now and as still as the wild. I can hear birds, the parlor maid coughing, and over by the lake a lot of crows. These are the nicest rooms in the house. It's an apartment over the porte-cochere; a big panelled study with a yellow chaise longue and an empire desk, busts of Brutus and Horace, bound volumes of *Punch* from 1833 to 1891, leaded windows, drinking horns, pewter steins, throne chairs, a ditto bedroom and stained glass windows in the bath."

My father loved to tell stories about the Trask family and their Yaddo. Although Katrina Trask had been a writer herself, he never mentioned this. Instead he told about Spencer Trask, a Wall Street genius, an investor in electricity and the *New York Times*, who was killed in 1909 on his way from Yaddo to New York after Christmas when his sumptuous private railroad car collided with a freight train that had been shunted onto the wrong track at the Harmon Yards. After that, George Foster Peabody, a southern gentleman who had been Trask's business partner, moved into Yaddo and became its head of household. Peabody had always loved Katrina, my father said, but it was not until 1921, after they had been living together at Yaddo for more than a decade, that they were finally married — and she died less than a year later. Peabody was an inspired philanthropist, and he took on the task of turning Yaddo's estate and assets into the haven for artists, writers, and composers that his wife had dreamed about. Later he fell in love with Marjorie Wait, a young divorcée, and because he could not marry her in the church, he adopted her. Marjorie's sister, Elizabeth Ames, was chosen by Peabody to become the new colony's director after a ray of light seemed to cast a halo around her at their first meeting. God couldn't have made a better choice. A bronze plaque in the music room at Yaddo commemorates the philanthropist with the words: "George Foster Peabody, Lover of Men." This became a great joke at Yaddo, my father said, as the implications of the phrase shifted through the years.

✳   ✳   ✳

After breakfast at Yaddo everyone repairs to their offices and studios for the day. There are no visits, no domestic chores, and no telephone calls, and lunch is a solitary picnic packed in a black metal lunch box by the staff each morning. This protection from the distractions of everyday life makes Yaddo a wonderful place to concentrate — an ideal atmosphere for a working writer — and of course that is the reason my father kept going there year after year for the rest of his life.

But Yaddo meant much more to him than even that. The place has the kind of eccentric class, old-fashioned servants, and grassy elegance that my father's soul required. When he went down the great stairs or strolled across the lawn to breakfast at the mansion, Nellie Shannon, the cook, would welcome him, take his order for eggs and bacon, and then lead him to the broad window to see how white the roofs were from the year's first frost, or where the forsythia was going to blossom at the edge of the path down to the rose gardens. He was a special guest at Yaddo, the servants' friend, Mrs. Ames's surrogate son. Sometimes he signed his letters from Saratoga "Little Lord Fauntleroy." Yaddo offered all the privileges of property but none of the responsibilities of ownership. And he didn't have to take it seriously, either. There were always hats on the statues at Yaddo.

My father found places like Yaddo all his life. Places where there were faithful servants and breakfast orders and ponds for swimming and velvety sloping lawns with big trees. Places he could enjoy without owning them. Treetops, my mother's family's place in New Hampshire, was like that, and so was Beechwood, the Frank A. Vanderlip estate where we lived from 1951 to 1960 in a little house that had once been a workshop. My father was always a visitor, a tenant. Perhaps he didn't want to be bothered with owning things, or maybe he felt he didn't deserve them. There was a practical problem as well: Until the 1960s he never made enough money to afford much elegance of his own. But at some level my father was always the homeless boy, the outsider, the one who stood at the edge of "respectable" life looking critically but wistfully in at his friends and neighbors.

It didn't make much difference that in 1960, when he was almost fifty years old, he was finally able to buy his own house, with ponds and velvety lawns and big trees, in Ossining, New York. His anxiety equaled his euphoria. For years he roamed the house at night, convinced that it was about to burn down, or break down somehow, or just vanish into thin air. At the same time, he never stopped enjoying other people's property. Although a swim was the center of his summer days, he didn't build a swimming pool of his own, even when he could have afforded to. He preferred to swim at Beechwood, in the marble-lined pool, with the ivy-covered walls and the statue of Mowgli, that William Welles Bosworth had designed for the Vanderlips; or at the Swopes', where an Italian fountain poured water down a falls into the shallow end and the pool was at the top of a ridge with views of the Hudson River and the Tappan Zee; or at Sara Spencer's, where the lawns swept up from the pool to a sylvan pond and there were Magrittes in the pool house; or at the Benjamins', where he could talk to Bud about his job as producer of CBS News; or at the Thaws', where a pair of Great Danes bounded out to meet him from the Stanford White portico. He was always welcome. "Oh John," people would say as his battered brown Volkswagen pulled in through their wrought-iron gates and up their gravel drives; "oh good, it's John."

Because of Yaddo, my father came to love the town of Saratoga Springs, and he made many friends there. He knew the president of the bank and the president of Skidmore College and most of the local bartenders. It was one of the places where he thought he might settle down with his young fiancée and raise a family.

"Everyone asks me if I'm going to come up here to live," he wrote my mother. "If you liked the place it would be a possibility. It's a raucous, genial, half-town, half-big-city. Main Street on a windy night is a lonely and desolate place, but there are at least five cozy bars full of civilized people. The race track has left this whistle stop with a lot of urbane graces. Rents are low, and credit at the grocers' seems to be inexhaustible."

Although my mother's reply to this letter has not been preserved, the fact that the subject didn't come up again for almost thirty years may be some indication of the enthusiasm she had for living in a small town where my father's connections would be their principal society. My father didn't give up, though. In the spring of 1959, after he had won the National Book Award for *The Wapshot Chronicle* and after we had returned from living for a year in Italy, my parents started looking for a house of their own. They didn't have much money, but mortgage rates were low and their expectations high. My father found a house he loved in Saratoga Springs. It was a run-down frame mansion on Union Avenue, with big upper rooms and bow windows and porches and even a porte-cochère. The president of the bank reviewed my father's finances, examined the house, and offered the necessary mortgage.

The whole family drove up to Saratoga one sunny spring day to see our new home. My mother looked carefully at the tree-shaded street where we would live. Many of the neighboring piles were falling down, some had been turned into boarding houses, and a few had big For Sale signs stuck in their weedy lawns. She examined the peeling paint in the graceful downstairs rooms and she stood in the tiny antique kitchen. She clocked the four-hour drive that would separate her from her friends and inquired about the all-day train trip to New York City. We had a cup of tea with the house's owners in the decrepit front parlor. My mother was very polite. We didn't move to Saratoga Springs.

My father often told me that after we had driven back from Saratoga that day, my mother turned to him as we were getting out of the car in Scarborough and said, "Please don't ever mention that house to me again." It probably wasn't that dramatic. It usually isn't. And a few months later my father fell in love with another old house with flagstone terraces and broad porches and lawns and big trees in Ossining, just a few miles north of the little house at Beechwood where we were living.

The last time I was at Yaddo was in 1976, when my brother Fred and I went up for the day to visit my father, who was working on his novel *Falconer*. It was early September, and in Saratoga the cool of autumn and the smell of apples were already in the air. We all larked around the main house at Yaddo, and my father showed us the music room and the fountains and the plaque to commemorate Mr. Peabody. Allan Gurganus — a student of my father's who had become a friend — was there, and the writer

Nora Sayre, and my father told us stories about the fun they used to have at Yaddo when he was young, and about the night he and Josie Herbst got drunk and dragged Mary Heaton Vorse down the great staircase in one of Katrina Trask's ornamental troikas with Mary shouting "Hooves of Fire!" We walked outside and down the lawns to the rose garden, we toured the artists' studios, and we visited Vincent the caretaker and his wife in their apartment over the garage. They beamed at us and pressed sweet drinks into our hands.

After that we got into the battered Volkswagen and drove around the little town. My father pointed out the new outdoor theater, and the highlights of the Skidmore campus, and his friend the president's house, and the Adirondack Savings Bank, and the house on Union Avenue that we almost bought and lived in. Union Avenue is prosperous now. The house has been perfectly restored and shines with new paint like the other houses behind the neat lawns and hedges. Rich people live there. Later in the evening, after dinner in the paneled dining room, we went out to visit the music studio that's in a stone tower that used to be the Trask family chapel, and a young composer played Chopin for us as the twilight darkened into night.

Four

My FATHER WAS a short man. In middle age, alcohol bloated his body and puffed up his face. When he stopped drinking for good in 1975, his weathered skin settled back onto bones so delicate that any of us could have easily picked him up — if we had dared. Physical contact was not encouraged in our family. On parting, we aimed kisses at one another's cheeks, and there were brief hugs for special occasions. We shook hands a lot.

But in spite of his actual height, my father must have had the carriage and facial expressions of a tall man, because people who had only seen him in photographs were often surprised when they met him. He had straight, fine brown hair that turned gray in his fifties, although he never looked like an old man. In fact, neither of my parents ever even looked really grown up — and neither do their children. Seen from a distance, as he rode his bicycle or spaded rows in the vegetable garden, my father always looked like a young man. Although he had sons of his own, he was always very much a son himself.

Clothes were important to him, and by the end of his life he had developed an aristocratic casual style that reflected his personal horror of vanity in men. This collided with his sharp sense of the importance of appearances. He didn't like to be caught looking in a mirror, and he felt that men shouldn't think too much about their hair or their clothes. They should, nevertheless, always look terrific. It was an eccentric double standard that reflected his rigid and con-fused ideas about correct masculine behavior. It also re-flected his fear of feminine behavior in men. Sometimes his shirts were frayed, or his sweaters out at the elbow, or his shoes down at the heel, because men didn't bother about such things. But he never would have worn a soiled shirt or gone a day without shaving — *that* would have been sloppy.

He had a Yankee face, with bright blue eyes, puffy eye-lids, and narrow lips, but his smile was so complete and so friendly that it changed his whole expression. As his fame increased, he developed another smile for cameras and peo-ple he didn't especially want to talk to. This smile left out his eyes and involved exposing his lower teeth. He had a kind of tense *heh, heh, heh* laugh that went with it. No one except his family could ever tell the difference, as far as I could see.

Although he was never wealthy (his income at the end of his life was about $150,000 a year, but for most of his life it was closer to $15,000), my father apparently had a manner that suggested breeding and money, at least to journalists. Many of the stories about him refer to his hunting dogs, his elegant country estate, his staff, his saddle horses. There were never any horses. There was never a staff. We did let our pet dogs have two litters of puppies while we were chil-dren, but the hunting dogs my father had in the 1970s and 1980s were a couple of hand-me-down golden retrievers who could barely be persuaded to return a tennis ball. The house in Ossining is charming, but after my parents bought it in 1960 for $37,500 (a combination of borrowed money, savings, and the wages of three weeks' work in Hollywood), the grounds fell into depressing disrepair. The big pond under the willows silted up and became a swamp. The ducks were eaten by neighborhood dogs, and their miniature house collapsed. The brook choked up and the ornamental bridges crumbled. Wisteria vines grew up the fruit trees in the orchard, the yew hedges went wild, and the stone walls disintegrated. It was all they could do, financially, to keep the house in working order.

My father was the first to admit that he was no landed aristocrat. He joked about the dogs' incapacities and laughed about being so broke he had to chop his own wood and do his own painting. Maybe people thought this was just a gentleman's underestimation of his own assets — more good breeding. Maybe that's what he meant them to think.

※　　※　　※

I was first aware that my father had an unusual accent when I started bringing school friends home to visit. Is your father English or something? they would ask. Why does your father talk that way? My father's accent must have developed from his Yankee father and his English mother and his childhood on Boston's South Shore, but out of these strains he developed a way of speaking that was unique, beyond accent, entirely his own. It was a clipped mumble, a combination of swallowed words and low laughter, short *a*'s and broad Yankeeisms. People outside the family often had difficulty understanding him. He said "dawl" for "doll" and "idear" for "idea," but it was much more than that.

The best illustration I know of his unique way of speaking, and the difficulties it presented, came up when I was tape-recording his answers to my questions for an interview that ran in *Newsweek* when he was on the cover after the publication of *Falconer* in 1977. I was an editor at *Newsweek* at that point, a job I was very proud to have, and the situation made me extremely nervous. I would either lose my job or my father's friendship before the interview was edited and published, I was sure. I composed a list of questions. My father also composed a list of questions — questions he thought I should ask him — along with their answers.

I interviewed him one rainy winter afternoon, in front of the fire in the downstairs living room of the house in Ossining. The dogs behaved themselves. My mother peeled shrimp in the kitchen for dinner while we talked. When I asked about Grandfather Cheever's lost money, my father told me that the stocks my grandfather had bought after selling Whitteridge and Cheever were his anchor to windward. The interview was professionally transcribed — there were five hours of tapes and very little time — and during this process "his anchor to windward" became "Yuzanka the Wounded."

In spite of my fears, the interview came out well, in *Newsweek* terms at least. I didn't get fired. My father and I stayed friends. *Falconer* was number one on the best-seller list, and my father even wrote me a thank-you note, slipped into an envelope along with a press release about the *Newsweek* cover. "The lesson let us help one another was not lost on you," it said.

Now, reading over the sixty or so pages of transcribed tapes, I am struck for the first time by the humor and sadness of the questions my father had prepared for me to ask, and his answers.

Q. Did you marry and have children in order to have material for your work?

A. No, of course not. I'm married to your mother because I love her, and having children was an expression of our life together. But the question does bring up the difference between reporting and . . . fiction. Fiction is conscientious to what most closely resembles our dreams. Journalism is conscientious to the available facts.

Q. Do you think that the children of writers are destined to lead tragic and sorrowful lives?

A. No, I don't think it should affect them. I do not think wealth of talent should affect children any more than any other kind of wealth. It seems to me that dealing with plenty and abundance is extremely difficult, and one sees this in the children of rich men. It seems to me that anything you don't do yourself is very hard to handle. Any fame that comes to you, any money that comes to you, any talent that comes to you, you can't feel you've won yourself.

My father used to say that since the Cheevers were a seafaring family, keeping ship's logs or journals and writing in general were a part of our tradition. My grandfather kept a journal of loose-leaf notebooks filled with reports of the weather, his memories of his youth, and his physical condition. My father's journal is typed on the same kind of loose-leaf pages, in small notebooks bound in black or blue — depending on what the local stationery store was stocking. Sometimes he wrote long entries every day. Sometimes he skipped weeks and months. The entries aren't dated, and there are no clues to guide the reader. The narrative shifts from recollection to fiction without notice. There are about thirty volumes in all, now — sections of the journals seem to have been lost or destroyed — and they include everything from descriptions of landscape and weather, his childhood, his marriage, and ideas for stories to philosophical perorations on alcoholism, sexuality, and the act of writing.

You have been lost in a wood. When you realize that you are lost the mind is instantly animated with a kind of stoic cheerfulness. How much worse it could be, you think. You have warm clothes, dry matches and half a cup of water left in the canteen. If you have to spend two or three days out you will surely survive. You must avoid panic. You must keep your eyes and your mind in the most accommodating and relaxed condition. Within an hour your calmness is rewarded. There is the trail! A new kind of blood seems suddenly to be let into your heart. Your strength and your mind are refreshed and off you go . . . If you keep to a decent pace, you will be back to the shore where the boat is by dark. You hold to the pace. You keep your eye sharply on the thread of trail. You do not stop . . . You hike until the end of the afternoon and seeing that the light has begun to go you stop to see if you can pick out the noise of the waves that you should, by now, be able to hear. The place where you stop seems to be familiar. You have seen that dead oak before; that wall of rock, that stump. Then you look around. There is that heavy creel that you discarded at noon. You are back at the point where you discovered that you were lost. The lightness of your heart . . . was illusory. You are lost; and it is getting dark . . . This is the situation in which I find too many of my characters. I never seem to be able to bring them out of the woods on the one hand, or to transform the world into a forest.

The journals are short on everyday details. These were the pages where he could improvise, experiment, and refine. He had a roster of fictional names and personalities that he wove around his family and friends and used in his journals, and more than half a dozen names for himself, or the characters that had originally been based on himself: Toby, Tom, Streeter, and Bierstubbe, or Mr. Bierstubbe, to mention just a few. The journals were also the arena in which he wrestled with his personal demons — alcohol, sex, and his acute sense of what he might have done wrong. These were bloody

battles. He was down so often that he had a dozen words for
it: cafard, the megrims, depresh, the blues, low again. In the
journals, incidents he made into the comic stories he loved
to tell about his life are often revealed as upsetting or
humiliating. Between my father's perception of his life and
his verbal accounts of his life, pain is transformed into
humor.

The journals were private, of course, kept as a record of
ideas and descriptive phrases as well as a means of writing
some kind of order into pain and chaos. But toward the end
of his life, after he stopped drinking, my father realized
what an extraordinary document his journals had become,
and I think that he meant them to be read some day. He
hauled them out of their boxes in the attic, or off the shelves
at the top of his clothes closet, and encouraged us to read
selected passages from them. He sent a section off to the
Brandeis University library, and promised another for a
small printing at the University of Alabama. He tried for a
while to find a university or a major library collection that
would take them under his complicated stipulations, and
he was pleased by the fact that people who read parts of the
journals were shocked — both by their vigor and their indiscretion.

One of the constant themes in the little notebooks is his
increasingly desperate effort not to drink so much. Over two
decades, they chronicle his change from a dashing, hard-
drinking writer, in a world where many of his friends
polished off two martinis before lunch, to a dilapidated, com-
pulsive, suicidal alcoholic, in a world where a lot of people
drink only white wine and mineral water. He hated himself
for drinking even more than for other things. It obsessed
him. It turns out that often when he seemed cranky and I
wondered why, he was just waiting for me to leave the room

so he could have another whiskey. Not that I would have noticed; he seems to have needed the secret almost as much as he needed the drink. Long before I was even aware that he was alcoholic, there were bottles hidden all over the house, and even outside in the privet hedge and the garden shed. Drink was his crucible, his personal hell. As early as the 1950s, when he was struggling to write his first novel, *The Wapshot Chronicle* (which was finally finished in 1956, when he was forty-four), he spent a lot of energy trying not to drink before 4 P.M., and then before noon, and then before 10 A.M., and then before breakfast. But the alcohol hadn't blurred his acuity or softened his critical vision in those years the way it did later.

"And at 3 A.M. I seem to be walking through Grand Central Station," he wrote in 1956, the year I was thirteen. "And the latch on my suitcase gives, spilling onto the floor the contents of my life and what do we find there? A pint of gin and some contraceptives; the score for Handel's *Water Music* and a football; the plays of Shakespeare, *The Brothers Karamazov* and *Madame Bovary*; a sweater and a jockstrap and an old maddar necktie; but also, to signify times of irresolution and loss about which I know plenty, a daisy for counting and a candle for impotence; but also a hairbrush and a love poem and a photo of happy times on the deck of the tern and a yellow leaf or some such — a stone from the beach to signify times of solid high spirits."

❊   ❊   ❊

Late at night the telephone rings. My father has been dead six months, but the ringing phone reminds me of the late-night calls I got when he was sick, and of the call I was expecting then but never got because I was with him when he died. Now the call is from a writer my father encouraged for a while and finally gave up on. He always drank too much. His career never confirmed the promise of his early work. Through the low static of the long-distance connection, I can hear the sound of other voices in the background and the tinny music of a juke box playing.

"I have these letters from John," this writer says. His voice is slurred and slow. "He wrote me these letters. I don't know why he told me these things."

"What kind of things?" I say. His glass clunks against the mouthpiece of the telephone.

"Terrible things. I don't know why he told me. I wouldn't ever publish them, of course."

"Why don't you send me copies and I'll have a look?"

"I mean I know John cared about me, but I don't know why he wrote me these letters if he didn't want me to use them somehow, you know?"

"I can't know until I see them," I say. I do know the law. No one can publish letters without the permission of the letter writer's estate. My mother is the executor of my father's estate.

"I wouldn't want Mary to see these, I didn't want to bother her," he says. The background music seems louder. I can hear someone else asking to use the phone. "I don't know," he says. "It's dough, you know. I don't have any. I could get some dough for these. I mean if he didn't want me to use them, why did he write me these letters?"

"I doubt that he meant you should sell them," I say. It is dark in our bedroom. Outside I can see the streetlights on Central Park West and the shadows of the big trees in the park. "What's in these letters?" I ask. "What are they about?"

"Awful things, about his brother, and Mary, and I wouldn't want Mary ever to see them," he says. His voice sounds high and anxious now. "I just can't figure out why he wrote me these letters if —" There is a series of clicks, and our conversation is cut off. I hang up and sit for a moment on the edge of the bed wondering where he was calling from, what dingy bar in what far-off city. And I wonder what could be in those letters, and why my father might have written secrets to a man he never trusted. It's late at night. After a while, I go back to sleep.

Five

My FATHER FIRST SAW my mother when he stepped into the up elevator at 545 Fifth Avenue on a warm autumn afternoon in 1938. He had been in New York almost a decade by then, and he was steadily selling his stories to Harold Ross and Gus Lobrano at *The New Yorker* as well as to half a dozen other magazines. He was writing a novel. He had spent a year in Washington, D.C., working on the WPA guidebook to New York City, collecting his first regular paycheck, going to parties, falling in and out of love, and buckling up his shiny new pair of jodhpur boots with crossed straps to ride the horses at Fort Belvoir. He had his own apartment in Greenwich Village, and he was established as a regular at Yaddo. Although he had never landed an editorial or staff job on a magazine, it was becoming clear that he could make a living as a writer. In retrospect, my father's career seems a straight, certain line, confidently directed toward writing fiction, but in fact he tried very hard to get regular jobs, and he tried to write at least one long nonfiction piece for *The New Yorker*. It was circumstance as well as determination that made his focus so clear, and he paid a high price for it. He was never relaxed about money, although he gallantly and sometimes frantically pretended not to care. One day he would feel rich, the next day he felt poor. He hated debt, and poverty depressed him.

When he stepped into that fateful elevator in 1938, he was a young writer on his way to see his literary agent, Maxim Lieber. He always said that he would have followed my mother anyway, but as it turned out, he didn't have to. She too was on her way to Lieber's office, where she had found a job after graduating from Sarah Lawrence College. And that, according to my father, was that.

My mother remembers their meeting a little differently. It was a rainy day, she says, and my father wore a brown tweed coat that was so much too big that the sleeves came down over his fingertips. On their first date, he didn't have enough money to pay for dinner. It was obvious that he needed someone to take care of him.

But he was a twenty-six-year-old who knew what he wanted, and for that moment there was no resisting him. My mother had little reason to resist. This pattern — my father as the alternately pursuing and rebuffed, resentful male, and my mother as the passive, coerced, resentful female — was held to as long as they were together. At any rate, my father moved in next door to my mother's apartment in Rhinelander Gardens, a row of Greenwich Village houses that was torn down in the 1950s. After they were married, they set up housekeeping in a two-room apartment at 19 East Eighth Street, near Fifth Avenue.

They married in March of 1941, and they stayed married for more than forty years — a constancy that seemed alternately noble and ludicrous. Why they chose to remain faithful to the final vows of the marriage ceremony is more or less a mystery. They certainly didn't remain faithful to each other. Sometimes they made each other so miserable, especially in the 1960s and 1970s, that their divorce would have been a relief. Maybe it was habit that kept them together, maybe it was perversity, maybe it was love — a kind of love so different from what we mean by love these days that there should be another word.

Often enough, just as we three children were convinced that the end of the marriage had arrived, they would reconcile and turn on us in disbelief. "But I *adore* your mother," my father would say in a tone of voice that implied that only a crazy fool could have doubted this essential truth. And she would show off a new bracelet or string of beads he had given her and smile seraphically. I imagined bringing a divorce lawyer out to their house in Ossining (they both repeatedly asked us to find them good lawyers), only to discover them holding hands and giggling like teen-agers. Then, just as I thought they might finally be settling down with each other — they were getting old, after all! — my mother would take me aside and explain that he was impossible and selfish and she couldn't bear to live with him anymore. Or my father would announce that he had put up with her coldness long enough and that he was in love with a movie actress, or a painter he had met at Yaddo, or a student from one of his writing classes who thought he was wonderful.

I think my father had a fear of being predictable. Never was a fear less justified. He would often assure us that he and my mother were *not* going to have a cozy, greeting-card old age together, and he made unmerciful fun of any kind of marital complacency. My mother's attitudes were equally unconventional. In her collection of poems, *The Need for Chocolate*, which was published in 1980, a woman addresses her husband in a poem called "Gorgon I":

I have sometimes complained, husband,
that as you feinted, shadowboxed and blindly
jived to that misty monolithic woman in your mind
I have been battered, drowned under your blows.

There is a row of white wooden columns across the front porch of the house in Ossining my parents bought in 1960. This was their home, I guess you could say, although my father threatened to sell it for financial reasons almost as often as he or my mother threatened to move out. I used to imagine my parents' complaints about each other as an operatic scenario, with the porch as the stage set. He would take me behind one column and complain that she had rejected him. She would take me behind another column and complain that he had never understood her. In between, they would go *pssst, pssst, pssst* behind their hands to the audience. Two duets.

My mother's family background was enough to make my father's look like a Norman Rockwell all-American childhood. Her father, Milton Charles Winternitz, was a brilliant doctor and teacher whose temper tantrums while he was the dean of Yale Medical School were famous here and abroad. He was a short, innately elegant Jewish man from Baltimore, Maryland, whose family had emigrated from Austria before the turn of the century. Although my grandfather liked to say that he had been an impoverished guttersnipe, his father had in fact been a middle-class doctor who treated Baltimore's poor using the simple medical techniques of that time. My grandfather didn't intend to follow in his father's plodding footsteps. By the age of sixteen he had earned his own medical degree from Johns Hopkins, where he had also met his future wife, Helen Watson, a beautiful woman from a wealthy and eccentric Protestant family, and one of the first females to earn a medical degree in this country.

While he was in his thirties, my grandfather was dispatched from the teaching staff at Hopkins to oversee the modernization of the medical school at Yale. He was dean of Yale Medical School at the age of thirty-five, and he held the position for fifteen years. He retired from the deanship in 1935, although he continued as professor of pathology. Terrifying and demanding in the classroom, he was able to hone his temper into an effective teaching device. No one ever forgot him, and no one ever forgot anything he taught them. He could be fabulously generous or brutally cruel. His personality was so intense that even now, more than twenty years after his death, I occasionally meet doctors who were his students or his colleagues and it becomes clear, as we talk, that he was the driving force in their careers. Everyone either hated or loved my grandfather. My father loved him.

By the time my parents met, my mother's mother had died after a long illness, leaving five young children. *Her* father, Thomas Augustus Watson, had been Alexander Graham Bell's friend and assistant; they invented the telephone together. When Bell excitedly called out "Mr. Watson, come here!" because he had spilled acid on his hand, and the words were transmitted to the next room, it was my great-grandpa Watson who came running. After a life of satisfying his adult whims, during which he spent most of the money that was his share from the invention, Grandpa Watson died in 1934; but his wife, my great-grandma Watson, was an old dragon who was still alive when I was a child. I remember my great-grandmother as a stern woman in a long black dress and high-button shoes with a neat bun of white hair. Her image is a nice curb for my tendency to be nostalgic about the past. "Children should be seen but not heard" was her favorite dictum.

My mother was twelve when her mother died, and her father soon met the woman who was to become his second wife. The way the story goes, Grandfather Winternitz was driving somewhat distractedly through New Haven when he ran right smack into Mrs. Pauline Webster Whitney's Studebaker. They both got out of their cars to survey the damage. "Oh," said Mrs. Whitney, who knew just about everything that went on in New Haven. "So you're Doctor Winternitz from the medical school who's supposed to be *so smart*."

Mrs. Whitney, or Polly, as everyone called her, already had four children by her late husband Stephen Whitney. (After she married my grandfather, they had nine between them.) Fortunately, she loved children — although what loving children meant in that era of servants, nannies, and "mamselles" is a little obscure. The Whitney children were tall, fair, and blue-eyed, with high, trilling laughs and drawling upper-class accents. Their names were Louisa, Janie, Freddy, and Stevie. The boys drove roadsters and made conquests. The girls came out. My mother and her four brothers and sisters were not like that at all. They were dark-haired, intensely serious, and dedicated to the proposition that intelligence could conquer the world — their father was the example. Their names were Tom, Jane, Elizabeth, Mary, and Bill.

When my grandfather married Mrs. Whitney, she and her children moved into my grandfather's house — which she had thoroughly redecorated — near the Yale campus at 210 Prospect Street. Forced up against their opposites by my grandfather's passionate and capricious love for a woman they couldn't understand, the Winternitz children sometimes felt humiliated and diminished. The Whitneys were a few years older, and this made their sophisticated airs even harder to take. At worst they were mocking and bitchy, at best they were patronizing. The clash between these two sets of children has caused reverberations right down to the third generation. Even after they all left home (the Whitneys married Griswolds, Hotchkisses, and Langs, the Winternitzes married people named Primak and Mellors, Thompson and Cheever), the stand-off between the two parts of the family continued every summer, when the entire tribe, with wives, husbands, children, and baby sitters, went up to stay at Treetops, the hillside scattering of summer cottages that Great-grandpa Watson had built above Newfound Lake, New Hampshire, in the 1920s.

It was to Treetops that my father came courting my mother the summer after they met. "That was the summer that Joe Louis fought Harry Thomas and the Philadelphia Athletics won the pennant," my father wrote Malcolm Cowley years later.* "Stocks dropped six and one half million. Shoe designers featured a wedge heel. Battleship won the Aintree. Poisoned drink killed three at the Tewksbury Infirmary. The Whitneys played Mah Jong that summer in New Hampshire. White Dragon, said Polly. Pong, said Louise. Oh, damn you, said Polly. Three bamboo, said Louise."

---

* In fact, the Yankees played the Cubs in the 1938 World Series, and it was the Yankees who won.

Six

For my father, the past was a seductive and dangerous place. Those who tarried in the comforting half-light of their own memories and achievements were rarely heard from again. He had seen writers paralyzed by early success, and writers unable to get beyond the bitterness of academic or critical failures. He had seen the emptiness of men and women whose chief distinction was their hallowed Boston ancestry, and he had seen his mother's use of the quaint, the antique, and the nostalgic diminish his own father.

My father never saved anything. He scorned all conservative instincts. He never kept carbon copies or photocopies, invariably sending his original manuscripts off in the mail as if nothing could matter less. Once in the 1930s a story he had sold to *Collier's* was lost by the post office. My father had already spent the money he'd been paid for it. Unperturbed, he just sat down and wrote the story over again. Mementos were for failures and old ladies. He kept what family photographs we had stuffed in a low cupboard that only stayed shut when a stool was wedged against the knob, and he could barely be persuaded to keep copies of his own books. If he liked a new book he had read, he often gave it away. If not, he threw it out. He answered all his letters, whether they were from ladies in Indiana or graduate students or Saul Bellow or John Updike or Harold Pinter or John le Carré. Then he threw them out or burned them, whether they were from ladies in Indiana or graduate students or Saul Bellow or John Updike or Harold Pinter or John le Carré. The incinerator behind the old stone wall in back of the kitchen in Ossining was often merrily ablaze with letters and manuscripts, journals, and old notes. One afternoon he fed the flames three-quarters of a short novel he had written about a man who swims across a suburban county from swimming pool to swimming pool. The pages he had left became the short story called "The Swimmer."

Papers that escaped the incinerator or the trash basket were often lost. My father never had a filing system, or filing cabinets, or even a proper desk. Manuscripts were stashed under beds or on closet shelves or shoved to the back of crowded drawers. Other papers were stuck in books or "safe places" that were soon forgotten. At the end of my father's life, we started trying to gather his papers together for the estate lawyers. Stock receipts and bank deposit slips, military-service records and insurance policies, an old power of attorney, and the deed to the house were all scattered in various desk drawers and cubbyholes or stuffed into the wall safe that had been built into the house in the 1920s. We sorted through everything, but there was never enough to compile a complete record for the tax lawyers and accountants. The worst of many crises was over my father's military-discharge papers. Mr. Wadsworth needed them, but nobody knew where they were. It took two days to locate them. The day before the funeral my husband finally yanked open one

of the downstairs desk drawers with the energy of frustration and revealed a hidden compartment with a mildewed
envelope from the United States Army folded away in one
corner.

A few weeks later my mother and I were sorting through
the upstairs desk drawers looking for a lost insurance policy.
She opened a small cupboard full of old china wrapped in
protective flannel bags, and two bundles of letters tied with
string fell out onto the floor. They were the letters my father
had written her before they were married — from Yaddo,
from New York, when she was at Treetops, and from Spear
Street in Quincy, when he was visiting his parents. Mixed
in with these were the letters he had written her during the
war, from boot camp at the Croft in Spartanburg, South
Carolina, from Camp Gordon, Georgia, and later from
Hollywood and Manila. Who knows why they were saved?
The paper is yellow and disintegrating at the edges, as if
they had been in a fire. The typing is faded and sometimes
illegible; but my father's voice is intact.

"I came in on an ammunition carrier Friday," he wrote my
pregnant mother at the end of a furlough in 1943.

The camp was deserted and the barracks had an attic smell
and the cockroaches were sporting with one another. It was
a beautiful spring evening, sad and clear and warm, and it
felt a little like coming here for the first time. "E" Company
didn't get in until ten o'clock last night. And last night I
went into town with Addis the agitator. Some people wanted
to meet me because I'm an author so I went there for dinner.
They were nice enough and after that we went to call on
the people who live in the southern mansion.

The southern mansion looked like everything in the books
from a distance, with a big white pillared porch, jasmine
and magnolia growing all around and banks of white and
red camellias along the walks. But as soon as you stepped

into the house you could see that it was about 1903 vintage with gas lights and mahogany panellings. The man we went to see had been transferred so we saw his wife and her baby and another baby she was taking care of for the woman in the next room. Every room, and there must be nearly thirty of them, had a soldier's wife and baby in it. A couple of the bathrooms have been changed into makeshift kitchens. It was very strange. You could hear babies crying and smell cooking and there was a grand staircase like Yaddo and family portraits and souvenirs of the Chicago exposition and a general air of decay and neglect, and it was raining and on the way out I cut some camellias with my knife and they look just like the ones you buy in New York. The women are camp followers after a year of this life. Like soldiers they possess nothing that can't be carried. When the division moves out they stand on the porch and wave good-bye and then wait for a telegram or a post card to find out where they're going to move next. "This baby was born in Albany," the girl we were visiting said, "and this baby was born in Columbia, South Carolina." But they are not people like us.

After boot camp, my father was sent to Camp Gordon, near Augusta, Georgia, where he was a private first class with E Company of the Twenty-second Infantry. My parents had been married just two years. On my father's first leave from boot camp in Spartanburg, they had gone to a hotel in Greenville, South Carolina, and soon after that my mother realized she was pregnant. My mother still remembers my father's intensity that weekend. Six weeks of basic training had worn him from wiry to skinny, and his nerves were so raw that he couldn't sleep. Camp Gordon was a big improvement. There were companions, and trips into town, and an occasional bottle of whiskey. Some people had even heard about *The Way Some People Live*, my father's first collection of short stories, which had been published in 1942.

Later in 1943, the book came to the attention of an officer

in the Signal Corps unit at Astoria, Queens, where the army made films for the troops and wrote propaganda. He was impressed, and just before I was born, my father was transferred to Astoria. For the first year or so of my life, he was able to live with us and commute to the war by subway. After that, the Signal Corps sent him to Hollywood, and finally he was issued a gun and shipped to Manila. Before he got to use it, the war was over. "A shy, compact figure in ill-fitting government issue, he was not a warrior to strike terror in the hearts of the enemy," his Signal Corps colleague John Weaver remembered in a 1977 article in the *Los Angeles Times*. Weaver became a good friend of his, along with other writer soldiers such as Irwin Shaw and E. J. Kahn, Jr.

If my father hadn't been shifted to the Signal Corps, I would hardly have seen him during my first years, and I might not have had a father at all. Soon after his move north, the rest of the Twenty-second Infantry got their long-awaited orders to ship out to Fort Dix and then overseas. E Company was blasted to pieces on the beach at Normandy.

My father didn't want to go with the Signal Corps, though. He wanted to see action. He wanted to stay at Camp Gordon and go overseas with his buddies from E Company — Streeter, and Addis the agitator, and Caleb Muse, the wispy southern farmboy who believed in ghosts and kept a pet chicken in the barracks boiler room. Although his transfer to the Signal Corps meant he could work on writing instead of peeling potatoes and polishing his boots, my father protested violently. The army didn't care, and that was no surprise. After more than a year in the infantry, my father understood what the army was about. It was about endless waiting for orders, the boredom of routine day after routine day, and the unspoken and somehow exhilarating fear that the orders might come and the routine be shattered. Army life wasn't much, but at any moment you might be called upon to die. In the meantime, marking time at Camp Gordon was so boring that you almost wanted to. There were repeated and lengthy applications for every furlough, every weekend off base. Nothing was ever granted until the last minute. The system was geared to obliterating the individual. My father's sense of being someone special earned him nothing but scorn and more KP. He peeled a lot of potatoes in the army.

My father told me later that although he had finally become a sergeant, he had never been able to get into Officer Candidate School because he had repeatedly failed the army IQ test. I always thought this was funny, since I knew that my father was one of the smartest men in the world. But reading over his letters to my mother from Camp Gordon, Georgia, it doesn't sound so funny. My father was never comfortable with success, but he took his failures very seriously. He ignored or mocked his good reviews and brooded over the bad ones. My mother's reports on their friends' promotions rankled. Money was very short. What was she spending it on up there in New York City? He was often too poor to make telephone calls, too poor to buy whiskey, too poor to afford the army privileges that some of the other men had.

But the mail was free for soldiers, and my father volunteered for personnel duties so that he would have access to a typewriter. (He never developed a legible handwriting.) He wrote dozens of letters, and mail call was the high point of every day. But the letter he talked about in the years after the war was the one he got from his New York friend E. E. Cummings. Cummings was almost twenty years older than my father, and he had driven an ambulance in World War I and written a wonderful book about it, *The Enormous Room*. "I too have slept in mud with someone's boot in the corner of my smile," he wrote, and in the letter he enclosed an autumn leaf and a five-dollar bill. The image of Cummings's elegant humor in adversity helped a lot. Oh, Cummings! He knew what it was like.

If Cowley was my father's first adviser, Cummings was his first model. He loved to tell stories about Cummings, his unimpeachable Boston background, his devastating way with women. Cummings had a master's degree from Harvard, and his parents had been close friends of the Jameses. He was the most generous of aristocrats and the most stylish of dissidents. He knew the importance of fighting for miracles as well as he knew the forks.

"Hey sweetie! Hey! Hey!" the whores in the old Women's House of Detention on Greenwich Avenue would call through the barred windows when his tall, patrician figure appeared walking out of Patchin Place toward Sixth. He knew them all by name.

My father loved to tell stories about Cummings, and I think his favorite was about the night the poet and his wife Marion — a former *Vogue* model — were leaving a swanky uptown New Year's Eve party and realized they didn't have enough money to take the subway back home to Greenwich Village. Cummings was usually poor, but it never would have occurred to him to worry about this during the party, and it didn't occur to him to think about it until they had said their good-byes and stepped into the mirrored elevator. Cummings and Marion were dressed in their shabby but superb evening clothes, looking like a couple of immortals with their tall bodies and their perfect bones, and they found themselves in the elevator with a portly Brooks Brothers type.

"Excuse me," Cummings said as the elevator started down. "Would you care to step on my hat?" With a regal sweep he placed his hat on the floor. The portly fellow was willing enough. Cummings's demeanor made everything seem possible.

"I'm afraid it will cost you five dollars," Cummings added, using his aristocratic accent to suggest it was a bit painful for two gentlemen to discuss money. The man stepped on Cummings's hat and paid his fee from a fat roll of banknotes. Cummings and Marion went home in a taxi.

I met Cummings when he came to give a reading at the girls' preparatory school where I was a sophomore. He was suffering from arthritis then, and too old to be doing small-town readings, but they brought him some money. My father and I appeared, unannounced, at the stiff little gathering in the headmaster's office before the show, and the two men embraced. The force and openness of their affection for one another seemed to shake that airless, heavily draped room. Cummings was so glad to see a loving face among those furnished souls that he could have wept, although he threw back his head and laughed instead. At the reading, his musical voice held the audience of girls spellbound, and he was called back for encores until he appeared for the last one in his muffler and coat. I sat with my father as Cummings read "my father moved through dooms of love," his elegy to his dead father. After the reading we drove him back to New York City in our secondhand car, and all the way he regaled us with hilarious accounts of his ride out — he had been doubled over so completely in the English teacher's sports car that he was sure he would be at least temporarily crippled. Cummings talked and told stories about visiting Russia, about visiting friends at Peter Cooper Village, and about the debilitating pain of his arthritis. He treated his pain with a fine mixture of humor and scorn.

When he talked about the world, it sounded like a wonderful place.

It was late at night when we turned off the East River Drive onto Houston Street, and we all had hamburgers together at the White Castle on Sixth Avenue, and then we dropped him off at Patchin Place and I never saw him again.

When people found out that my father was dying, some of them asked if I had read Dylan Thomas's poem "Do not go gentle into that good night." The poem is an invocation to Thomas's father not to give up life without a struggle: "Rage, rage against the dying of the light." It's a beautiful poem, and in the 1970s, when my father was dying of drink the way Thomas did, I used to play a record I have of Thomas reading it in his melancholy, melodious Welsh voice, and I used to weep.

But my father didn't die that way. When he did die, his illness seemed so unfair, so arbitrary and cruel, that I am sure it will take the rest of our lives for my family to understand how it could have happened. Instead of reading Thomas when my father was sick, I read Cummings's poem about his own father. It's a poem about a man who was so triumphantly alive that his death doesn't matter.

. . . .
 though dull were all we taste as bright,
 bitter all utterly things sweet,
 maggoty minus and dumb death
 all we inherit,all bequeath

 and nothing quite so least as truth
 —i say though hate were why men breathe —
 because my father lived his soul
 love is the whole and more than all

Cummings died in 1962 when he was sixty-seven, just about twenty years before my father died. It was at the end of the summer and still very hot, and he and Marion were staying at the house he had on Silver Lake in New Hampshire, near where the Jameses had lived, in the shadow of Mt. Chocorua. Marion was standing in the kitchen in the golden afternoon light that slants down onto the ferns through the birch and maple leaves there. My father liked to tell how she leaned out the window toward where Cummings was working and called, "Cummings, isn't it frightfully hot to be chopping wood?"

"I'm going to stop now, but I'm just going to sharpen the ax before I put it up, dear," Cummings said. And later, when she went out to find him, he was dead.

Seven

S USAN CALLS ME," my father wrote in his journal in 1952. "It is four or five in the morning. 'I have such awful thoughts, Daddy,' she says. 'I think there is a tiger in the hall and that he will eat me.' She laughs, but she is frightened. It is the hour before light. The dark is troubled for us both. There are no ghosts of men or tigers in the hall, but the dark is hard to bear. There will be great pain and labor before we see this obscurity transformed into sweet morning."

* * *

On a cold sunny Monday, about two months before my father died, I checked into New York Hospital and had my own first child, a daughter, Sarah. From the instant I saw her, a tiny red creature bathed in the weird underwater light of the hospital operating room, I loved her with an intensity that life had not prepared me for. As I had grown more pregnant, my father had become sicker. He lost a little every day, and that loss seemed to cast a shadow over all of us. The birth of the baby didn't take away that loss, but it changed everything for me.

My parents drove in to visit me at the hospital the day after she was born. My mother brought a calico mobile, I drank a glass of champagne, and my father's gaunt unbalanced face beamed in at Sarah's plastic bassinet through the transparent wall of the nursery. Her birth seemed to revitalize him. He called the next morning and told me that he felt much better. It was early, but the hospital was already awake. My room was filled with flowers. The cancer was finished, my father had decided. "I've kicked it, Susie," he said. "It's over."

It's a measure of human optimism that we all believed him. For a few weeks it even seemed to be true. He would never be well, of course, but the weakened, wasted father that was left seemed infinitely precious. My first postpregnancy outing was to see him receive the National Medal for Literature at Carnegie Hall. He looked frail, but he spoke with great strength. Afterward my husband and I went backstage. He wasn't there; we found him and the rest of the family ensconced on the banquettes of the Russian Tea Room next door, laughing and eating and ordering more. But early in May, when we took the month-old baby out to visit my parents in Ossining, he looked weaker.

"Make your famous baby noise, John," my mother urged him, and he curled up his lip in a comic high-pitched squeal. Then suddenly he seemed very tired. "Thank you for remembering, dear," he said. That's when I knew he was worse again. As the baby awakened to the world around her that first and last spring, my father waned and faded and grew more absent. The weather stayed warm and sunny. The cherry trees blossomed and shed their pink flowers like a snowfall on the paths in Central Park. The trees turned lush and green. Babies keep odd hours, and often as I watched the sunrise colors well up from the East Side while I fed my daughter, I thought of my father who might be lying awake in his bed in Ossining. In the evening when the baby slept, I called him. By that time, he rarely answered the telephone.

"He won't eat anything," my mother said. Her voice sounded ragged. "Here, Susie, you tell him he has to eat something."

"Hello," my father said in the normal voice that he still managed for telephone hellos and one-word answers.

"Hi, Daddy," I said. "I think you should eat something."

"Yes." His voice had subsided to a grating whisper, and the words were slow and drawn out. Sickness seemed to heighten his sense of social propriety. As his thinking became more chaotic, his manners became more impeccable.

"Shall I call you after dinner?" he said.

"Yes, Daddy." The receiver banged against the telephone as he dropped it.

I remember my father at the head of our family dinner table. First, when there were only three of us, he sat at the end of the plain pine table in the hallway that was the dining room of our apartment on Fifty-ninth Street in New York City.

Later, after we had moved out to Scarborough, he sat at the black modern table next to the window that looked out over the lawns toward Beechwood and the green metal garbage pails behind the estate's big garage. My brother Ben and I sat on opposite sides of the table. At breakfast, before we went to school, Ben would hold a napkin up to his face, slipping food under the bottom edge so that he wouldn't have to look at me. At dinner, nothing like that was allowed. I set the table and my mother cooked and brought the food out in serving dishes and we all sat down and my father said grace.

"Dear Lord, we thank Thee for Thy bounty," he would say while Ben looked longingly at the protection of his napkin. If we children were fighting, as we often were, my father would add a pointed, "And bless this table with peace." And if the dogs were grumbling for scraps under the table, he would also add, "both top and bottom." Then he would say "Amen." My father always said grace. Sometimes he stayed with the short and traditional, sometimes he improvised. Later on, for special occasions, he would base the grace on his favorite quotation, a paraphrase of a line from Jowett's translation of Plato: "Let us consider that the soul of man is immortal, able to endure every sort of good and every sort of evil." Then he would add a paraphrase of the words of the prophet Micah: "So let us live humbly and give thanks unto Our Lord God. Amen."

In the house at Ossining there was a long cherry dining room table with Italian wood and wicker chairs. I always sat on my father's left, with my back to the wall, facing the fireplace with the wing chair in front of it and the long bench next to it that was piled precariously high with galleys of new books and newspapers and magazines: that day's *New York Times*, the local *Ossining Citizen Register*, *The New Yorker*, *The New York Review of Books*, *Newsweek* (when I was working there), *Antaeus*, and sometimes *The Smithsonian* or the *Brown Alumni Monthly* — or anything else that had come in the mail recently enough to have avoided being thrown out. Sometimes at the table my head bumped against the frame of the Piranesi etching that hung on the wall behind me.

I went away to school in 1960, the year my parents bought the house, and Ben went off soon afterward. We three children were rarely there at the same time. When we were, my two brothers sat across from me on the same side of the table. The dogs warmed our feet, sometimes raising themselves for a halfhearted sally after one of the cats. At Christmas vacation, the porch outside would be piled high with snow. In the summer, delicious smells from my mother's flower garden wafted through the open top half of the Dutch door at the end of the room.

The family meal was always served onto our plates by my father from serving platters, and when everyone had said grace and we had all concluded "Amen," my mother would say, "Oh, John, you haven't left yourself anything but the carcass" (if it was a chicken), or "the head" (if it was a fish), or "the tail" (if it was a steak), or "the gristle" (if it was a roast). She was often right. My mother always felt that there wouldn't be enough for her family to eat. Food was so rich and so abundant in our house that even the pets were all overweight. My father, on the other hand, was convinced that somehow he would go hungry — that he would be left out, overlooked, not provided for. He usually managed to make *his* fears seem legitimate, even if it meant heaping our plates to the edges so that there wouldn't be quite enough left for him. "Oh, don't worry about me, dear," he would answer my mother. "This is plenty for me." We used to call him Eeyore.

The food, however, was not the main event at our dinner table. Conversation was the main event. Sometimes there was a general discussion of one person's problem: What would I do if Roddy Butler asked me to the dance at the country club? Should Ben major in English at school? Could Fred bring his friend Brad to New Hampshire? Advice, comments, and suggestions came from all quarters. Sometimes it was funny, sometimes it was friendly, sometimes it was

harsh or sarcastic. Someone would certainly point out that
Roddy had no intention of asking me anywhere, that Ben
would be lucky to *pass* English, and that Fred might have
trouble keeping his friends if he didn't learn to keep his
elbows off the table. There was a lot of joking and very little
serious counsel. We learned to make real decisions privately,
on our own. My parents' problems were rarely discussed,
because that usually ended in tears from my mother or
recriminations and sarcasm from my father — and nobody
got dessert.

Sometimes my mother or father would come up with an
image, or a fragment of a story, and we would all weave
imaginary plots around it. Sometimes we talked about books
or movies or the poetry we recited to each other on Sunday
afternoons. Often we talked and speculated about other
people, our neighbors and friends. No one ever hesitated
to be mean — although the insults were usually also pretty
funny. We were so mean to each other, in fact, that guests
were often astonished and shocked. They didn't catch the
undertone of humor in our quick sarcasms, and there were
times when we didn't catch it either. Explosions and tears
and sudden departures were not at all uncommon. My
brothers called our dinner table "the bear garden."

"My daughter says that our dinner table is like a shark
tank," my father wrote in his journal one day in 1970,
between a drunken lunch in honor of his friend Yevtushenko
and an evening spent brooding over a bad review of *Bullet
Park*. "I go into a spin. I am not a shark, I am a dolphin.
Mary is the shark, etc. . . . But what we stumble on is the
banality of family situations. Thinking of Susan, she makes
the error of daring not to have been invented by me, of
laughing at the wrong time and speaking lines I have not
written. Does this prove that I am incapable of love or can

only love myself? Scotch for breakfast and I do not like
these mornings."

         ❊   ❊   ❊

By Thanksgiving of 1981, my father was already too sick
to eat much. Of course we didn't know how sick. He had had
a kidney removed in June, and all summer he had seemed
to get better, but in the autumn, as the air cooled and the
leaves changed color, he seemed to be weaker again. When
Richard Avedon took a picture of him for the cover of
The Dial, the photograph looked stark and strange. He
couldn't ride his bicycle anymore, and so the doctor sent
him to a chiropractor. He went twice a week and installed
a primitive traction device on Ben's bed upstairs, where he
was working then. He wasn't working much, though. *Paradise* had been finished in the spring, and he spent most
of his time answering mail and keeping the journal.

My father never quite trusted medicine. On the one hand,
he always thought he was fine; at the same time, he always
knew he was dying. His perception of physical reality was
tenuous at best. Maybe his mother's Christian Science had
something to do with it, too. His solution was to stick to
small-town doctors and small-town hospitals, where at least
he was known and felt comfortable and where it seemed
they often told him what he wanted to hear. As a result,
when he needed sophisticated diagnosis and expert medical
care, he seemed to prefer jolly talk and home remedies. As
the pains in his ribs and legs got worse, he was often depressed.

It was the beginning of December by the time he went
back into the hospital for some X-rays. The shadows on
those heavy plastic sheets showed that cancer had spread
from his kidney up to his lungs and down into his legs; and

that was why he felt, as he put it, "so lousy." After they saw the X-rays, the doctors told him there was nothing they could do. There was no treatment. The cancer was too far along.

My husband and I were in La Jolla, California, visiting my husband's daughter that week. "It's very bad," my mother said when I called home to see how the X-rays had come out. "It's very bad." Her voice sounded strange. I was sitting on a bed in a hotel room in Southern California. There was a bureau with a few books on it, and my maternity clothes were thrown over a chair. The main street of La Jolla was outside heavily curtained windows.

"They say I'm a dying man," my father said. His voice was still strong, but the laugh in it seemed to fade as I listened. "They say that my bones look moth-eaten." There was an edge of irony to his voice, as if he were talking about someone else. The hotel room had been decorated in Spanish mission style, and the walls and the bedspread were orange. It was the end of the day. Downstairs, people were waiting to meet us for drinks in the Patio Bar. My father told me that my brother Fred would be flying home for the holidays. "Some people will do almost anything to get their children home for Christmas," he said. I leaned back against the headboard, and the ridges of molded wood dug into my spine. A painting of a cowboy hung on the wall. In the distance, I could hear the sound of the sea.

❋ ❋ ❋

"Oh," says a deep voice next to me. "Are you doing research on John Cheever?"

I look up from the big wooden desk and nod slightly. The New York Society Library has installed new lamps in the downstairs reading room, and their light reflects a pair of wide gray eyes.

"Did you read his first story, 'Expelled'? It was reprinted in *The New Republic* when he died, you know."

"How nice."

"It's a great story! It's all there, if you ask me. Everything that came later. What a writer!" The eyes sparkle with a manic enthusiasm for literature, especially posthumous literature.

"Thanks for letting me know." I close the volume of *Dictionary of American Biography* and stand up.

"I always thought he was so great. Much better than Bellow and Updike and people like that."

"Fiction is not a competitive sport," I say, replacing the volume and picking up my papers.

"These days everything is competitive. It's not like it used to be, you know. I'll see if I can find you a copy of that story."

"Oh, thank you, no." I move toward the door.

"Are you writing a biography of John Cheever?"

"I don't think so," I say.

"You should, you really should. He was so important. I think of him as the Howells of the 1980s. Howells was underrated too, you know."

I think about the rich and turgid textures of *A Hazard of New Fortunes* and *The Rise of Silas Lapham*. The detail, the dedication to realism, the neat moral lessons of the plots. I smile politely and leave the room.

Outside the library it's a hot summer afternoon. The streets are empty on the Upper East Side, everyone is at the beach. At the corner I pass the parking garage where I stood with my parents and my brother Fred and his wife one night after dinner at my apartment. I had walked down Madison Avenue arm in arm with my father, and when I told him that my husband and I were going to have a child, he laughed and flushed with pleasure. Going by the garage revives this moment, and I wonder why the crises of our lives always seem to unfold in parking garages or hotel rooms in strange cities or airports or cars stuck in traffic jams. I turn the corner and walk up Madison past the supermarket and the bank to the bus stop.

Eight

WHEN I WAS A LITTLE GIRL we lived in a brick apartment building at 400 East Fifty-ninth Street, about a block from Sutton Place and the East River and just across the street from the sooty, noisy rumble of the Queensboro Bridge. Our living room windows looked right out into the iron fretwork of the bridge's ascending roadway. To the east we could see the minarets at the top and the wrought-iron supports that turned into concrete columns as they went down into the bubbling, treacherous currents of the river. To the west there was a parking lot, and beyond it the trolley-car stop where we waited for the creaky blue cars with wicker seats when my father took me on trips downtown, or over to the Central Park Zoo.

There were two playgrounds near our apartment. The closest one was directly under the bridge, down the hill past the baseball field that's a tennis bubble now. From the swings, we looked right up into the innards of the bridge and saw the cars going by from underneath. That was where I went with my mother, and baby sitters, and with Mildred, our maid. The other playground was a block further away and in the other direction, on York Avenue at Sutton Place. Its manicured paths and immaculate sandbox grace a quiet brick terrace above the river. A large bronze statue of a boar gleams from being stroked by generations of tiny upper-class hands. The dirty growl of commerce and the bridge seem miles away. That was where my father took me to play.

In the afternoons when I got home from school, he and I used to walk across the bridge to where you could see the stairs winding down toward Welfare Island. The pedestrian walkway was a narrow construction of iron panels with a rickety guardrail. It shivered and clanked every time a car went by. From it we could look down and see the river, far, far below us, swirling and sucking between its narrow stone banks. One afternoon my tweed cap with the brim and chin strap blew off in a gust of wind, and Daddy couldn't catch it. We watched as it floated down, tumbling and spinning until it was a tiny speck lost in the eddying currents. It took a long time. After that, my father was afraid of bridges.

"He knew the symptoms," he wrote in his journal a decade later, when the fear had turned to panic. "As he approached the bridge [in the car] there would be an excruciating tightening of his scrotum, especially his left testicle and a painful shrinking of his male member. As he began to ascend the curve of the bridge it would become difficult for him to breathe. He could fill his lungs only by gasping. This struggle to breathe was followed by a sensation of weakness in his legs which would presently become so uncoordinated that he would legitimately worry about being able to apply the brakes. The full force of the attack came at the summit of the bridge when these various disturbances would seem to affect his blood pressure and his vision would begin to darken. Once he was over the summit there was some relief, but the seizure would leave him so weak and shaken that he had discovered he could not raise a cup or a glass to his mouth for an hour or two."

❋   ❋   ❋

It was the noise and clatter of the bridge outside our windows that finally drove us out of the city in 1951, but to me those years at 400 East Fifty-ninth Street were a golden time. The war was over and everything was ahead of us. I went to the Brearley School. I learned to do cartwheels. Over Christmas I was entrusted with the class white rat, and later I acquired an elderly hamster named Algernon Belasco. My father was becoming successful and my mother loved him. Money didn't seem to matter as much then as it did later. In the summers we went up to Treetops or stayed in country houses with old friends: the writer Hazel Hawthorne in Provincetown, Josie Herbst in Erwinna on the Delaware River, Margot Morrow at Seven Gates Farm on Martha's Vineyard.

In the morning when I went to school, my father would put on his one good suit and his gray felt hat and ride down in the elevator with the other men on their way to the office. From the lobby he would walk down to the basement, to the windowless storage room that came with our apartment. That was where he worked. There, he hung up the suit and hat and wrote all morning in his boxer shorts, typing away on his portable Underwood set up on a folding table. At lunchtime he would put the suit back on and ride up in the elevator. In the afternoons after school we took long walks — over the bridge or up the East River Drive or along Fifty-ninth Street toward Fifth Avenue. There was often a stop at the old Menemsha Bar on Fifty-seventh Street. I loved the imitation waterfall and the seafaring pictures on the walls. In the evenings my father told me bedtime stories: stories about Faustina, the little girl who brought her parents breakfast in bed and who loved to clean up her room and comb her hair, and stories about a rabbit named Pauline, and her deceitful cousin Cassius Rabbit and her adventures with the villainous Horace Walpole Rabbit. (My father had never forgiven Horace Walpole for writing that Henry Fielding was "perpetually disgusting.") The Pauline Rabbit stories were usually cliffhangers, but the good and true rabbits, led by Pauline, always just managed to triumph over Cassius's self-serving lies and Horace Walpole Rabbit's wickedness — although you could never be sure what would happen next time. After bedtime, my parents often dressed up and went out to parties. There were a lot of parties.

My father was drawn to strength. My mother is drawn to need and the sweetness of the needy. An injured animal, a waif, a person in trouble — all elicit overwhelming concern from her. She has nursed countless animals back to health, feeding them with eyedroppers, wrapping their shivering bodies in soft covers. A blue jay, a squirrel, our own dogs, all owed their lives to her. Later, when she became a teacher, it was the students who could not succeed in conventional ways who attracted her finest energies. My warmest memories of my mother are from times when I was sick, or in pain, or in some kind of trouble.

My father, by the way, would have nothing to do with discussions like this. He never spoke about feelings or allowed himself to speculate on the inner mechanics of the family. "I love you all equally," he would say, or "I adore your mother." People remember my father's candor. "Although his manner was reticent, there was nothing John would not say about himself," Saul Bellow recalled in his eulogy at my father's funeral. In a way, that was true. He would tell you exactly what he had done to this or that mistress in a room at the St. Regis or in a motel in Iowa, and he would tell you that *The New Yorker* had paid him less than $1,000 for a story, and he would tell you that he took two Valiums and drank a pint of gin every day before noon. That was different, though. He did not like to talk about how these things felt; he did not like to talk about human emotions. He did talk, often eloquently, about human behavior. Are they really the same? I don't think so. My father's intense concentration on what you can see and hear and smell and touch was at the core of his gift as a writer. He focused on the surface and texture of life, not on the emotions and motives underneath. In creative-writing classes, teachers always say that it is important to "show" and not "tell." My father's work describes the way people live, and the way he lived. It never tells.

Life in New York City became more complicated when my brother Ben was born in 1948. The apartment suddenly seemed too small, and the bridge much noisier. The baby Ben had a series of traumatic operations to remove a mole on his eye. Then he burned his foot on the humidifier that had been set up to relieve my asthma. The asthma was getting worse. I had been promised a pet dog if I stopped sucking my thumb. When I did and the dog arrived, the asthma intensified. The pediatrician decreed that I was allergic to dogs, and the puppy was taken away. The asthma continued. I had mumps and then measles. At night I woke up screaming from nightmares, terrible dreams in which the old yak from the Central Park Zoo appeared, menacing and silent, next to my bed.

While we lived in New York, my father would sometimes take the train out to Westchester to visit Jack and Ginny Kahn, and they often drove up to Fahnstock together to ski, or across the river to the slopes at Belleayre. Jack — E. J. Kahn, Jr. — was a staff writer at *The New Yorker*, and the Kahns were close friends of my father's army friend Irwin Shaw, who was writing a novel about his and Jack's war experiences. The Kahns lived in a squat white house in Scarborough, New York, which had been built as a workshop on Beechwood, the Frank A. Vanderlip estate. The house was small and close to the traffic on Route 9, but with it came the use of the estate, with its great lawns and trees and even an elegant swimming pool.

In 1950 the Kahns decided to move — they built a contemporary house for themselves about a mile north on Scarborough Road — and the little white house at Beechwood was for rent. After the increasingly cramped rooms of our apartment, the house seemed quiet and spacious. There would be a room with windows where my father could work, a separate bedroom for me, gardens that my mother could transform into horticultural masterpieces, and lots of outdoors where healthy children could run and play. My parents were interviewed by the Vanderlip family members who owned the house, and they decided to rent it; we moved there in the spring of 1951, after my second-grade year at Brearley, and I was enrolled in the Scarborough School, a small day school right on the Vanderlip estate.

During the ten years we lived in Scarborough, my father and I used to go visiting on weekend mornings. After breakfast we would drive over to Croton to see the Boyers, or to the Maxwells' in Yorktown Heights, or up Scarborough Road to the Kahns', or to the Spears' in Briarcliff, or over to the Swopes' on Hawkes Avenue, or around the corner of the estate to the Schoaleses', or even across the river to the Ettlingers' in Pomona. Don and Katrina Ettlinger were friends of the Kahns and the Shaws, and Don had been in the Signal Corps with my father. These visits to friends usually featured martinis and lots of laughter. I would sink into the sofa and bask in my inclusion in adult conversation. Sometimes I took a book along, or my guitar. Occasionally the grown-ups would politely ask me to play, and I would strum the major chords and warble songs of sudden death and careless love. After a few hours, we went home for lunch.

Once, when I was about fourteen, as we were coming back across the Tappan Zee Bridge from a particularly jolly morning at the Ettlingers', I noticed that the car seemed to be stalling. As we approached the curving superstructure at the center of the bridge, the stalling seemed to get worse. I looked over at my father and saw that his foot was shaking against the accelerator. He was very pale.

"Talk to me," he said.

"About what?" I noticed that his hands were trembling, too. The car bucked along, edging toward the guardrail at the side of the bridge.

"It doesn't matter, just talk."

"Well, I'm reading a novel that I like a lot," I said. We had passed under the superstructure by now and were on our way down the other side. The car veered back into the center of traffic and out again toward the guardrail.

"Go on," my father said.

"It's about a love affair. When he loves her she doesn't love him and when she loves him he doesn't love her. He writes her a lot of letters." I was reading *The Red and the Black*. Below us I could see the flat brown water of the Tappan Zee, and ahead of us the spires of Lyndhurst and

Marymount College came into view. "He wins her back and then he doesn't want her, but she keeps on loving him anyway," I said. We had reached the tollbooth at the end of the bridge. My father's breathing relaxed and the car moved smoothly up the exit ramp. We stopped at the light and turned north up Route 9 toward home.

Years after that, my father wrote a story about his fear called "The Angel of the Bridge." "I felt that my terror of bridges was an expression of my clumsily concealed horror of what is becoming of the world," he wrote in the story. He was troubled by the unhappiness of his friends, appalled at the rows of new houses going up where meadows and trees had been, disgusted by the substitution of freeways for country roads and fast-food burgers for home cooking.

That was what he called "the dark side." But his worst depressions were often lightened by his vision of what life could be. "It all came back — blue-sky courage, the high spirits of lustiness, an ecstatic sereneness," he wrote in the story, describing the way he felt after a harp-playing hitch-hiker dispelled his fear by singing as they drove across the bridge. "I offered to take her wherever she wanted to go, but she shook her head and walked away, and I drove on . . . through a world that, having been restored to me, seemed marvelous and fair."

Nine

BEECHWOOD IS A CONDOMINIUM NOW. The stately mansion's ninety rooms have been remodeled into three deluxe apartments. The great William Welles Bosworth ballroom where we used to take dancing lessons and play duets on the Steinway grands is a library for the condominium community. The bookcases have been replaced with mirrors. The driveway is called Beechwood Way, and a row of semi-detached units, "the Great Lawn houses," face the old hockey field next to the farm where Sam the gardener used to pen the sheep and grow tomatoes that tasted like summer. Further down the brook, where a rose arbor led across the lawn to the Schoaleses' house, is another row of units, "the Woodland Houses." The swimming pool has been restored for the new owners of "Westchester's most exclusive new residential setting," and past the big lawn where the sheep grazed under the dogwood trees there are two hard-surface tennis courts. The little white house where we lived from 1951 to 1960 is rented to an executive at IBM's world headquarters on what used to be the William Rockefeller estate in North Tarrytown. On weekend afternoons, we children used to wander down past the Schoaleses' house, through the woods to the fascinating burned-out foundation of Rockefeller's mansion Rockwood Hall. Other times we walked north along the Hudson River and the railroad tracks to an abandoned castle on a cliff above the water. A huge iron loop embedded in its parapet had supposedly held one of the chains that kept the British from sailing up the river during the Revolutionary War. The castle is gone now, and an apartment building commands the heights.

When we lived at Beechwood, old Mrs. Vanderlip was still alive, and she dominated the estate's fifty acres and six lesser buildings from her silk-curtained bedroom under the mansion's white cupola. She was a sharp, stooped *grande dame* who leaned on a cane, and her eyes seemed huge behind the lenses of her glasses. We would often meet her walking in her gardens or over the lawns in the evening, and we were invited up to Beechwood for dinner sometimes, or to attend the neighborhood dancing classes that Mrs. V. held in the grand ballroom. We children also spent hours crouched in the ornamental shrubbery spying on Beechwood parties, where women in evening gowns talked with suave men in dinner jackets in front of the fire in the downstairs parlor, or in the music room with its oil portraits and glass cases of antique instruments, or in the ballroom with the books and the grand pianos and the huge painting of Andromeda chained to a rock that Mrs. Vanderlip said was by a very famous painter named Van Dyck.

Living at Beechwood confirmed our family's special status in the world. We had the luxuries of the very rich — rolling lawns, a swimming pool, gardeners who doffed their caps — but we were tenants, scraping to get by. We were friends of the Vanderlip family, but we were not the Vanderlip family.

We lived at Beechwood, but our home was a little house behind a big garage. My parents made it very clear that these things were not important. Although we were often miserable about having no real home, we were also proud to be nomads. We all responded ecstatically to the extraordinary physical beauty of the lawns and great elms and beeches separated by patches of woodland and divided by a clear brook. Each season had its delights, and we were free to roam over the grass and through the gardens and daydream under the willow trees.

"The glory of these spring evenings in the valley," my father wrote in his journal. "The twilight glares on the wet stones of the terrace. For a second the wet blacktop road is as blue as heaven. Through the brush I see the glow of garish, metallic light. Then this goes . . . It begins to rain in earnest and the cold water clears my head. I stand at the screen door for half an hour (I'm busy I tell the children) watching this spring evening in which the dark is so slow to gather, in which a glow beats up through the gray rain from the lawns and flowering trees. I seem to try to decipher this. Similes yes, the elm like a piece of wooden lightning; but the heart of the scene is withheld as, in looking inwardly to our own motives, the key, the beginning, is something we will never see. Reading about the charge of the light brigade I shut my eyes and saw a flaming heart; good, I thought, since after all I might have seen a toad."

The mansion, like the Hudson Valley landscape, was an inescapable presence, a five-story clapboard landmark that we could see from almost every window of our house. Its center rooms had originally been built by a character named Mathias the Prophet in the nineteenth century, we were told. Mathias drove a chariot with six white horses and lived in the suite of bedrooms that became the nursery for the six

Vanderlip children (Virginia, Narcissa, Kelvin, Frank, Charlotte, and John). Above the nursery was a group of rooms under the eaves called the footman's attic, and it was from here that Mathias the Prophet's footman had crept downstairs to murder him one night after they had quarreled. On cold evenings you could still hear the homicidal servant's sinister tread as he slowly creaked down the steps to his master's bedroom. It always sent chills up my spine; when it happened, my friend Sarah Schoales (Virginia's daughter) and I used to shriek and run for the safety of the grown-ups. But Sarah's uncle Frank said it was just the old wood in the original part of the house pulling away from the newer wood in the cooling air when the temperature dropped on winter nights.

After Mathias, Beechwood was owned by a series of railroad barons and financiers who added more rooms and columns to its federal-style façade. In 1906, Frank A. Vanderlip, then a vice-president of the National City Bank of New York, bought it from a member of the Vanderbilt family. Vanderlip had grown up on a farm, and at first he was daunted by the grandeur of the place, but his fortune and his family soon grew into it, and within a few years he was the president of the bank and a very rich man. Isadora Duncan danced on the lawn, and Italian and French formal rooms and gardens were purchased entire from defunct European castles. Herbert Hoover and Woodrow Wilson came for dinner, as did Vanderlip's colleague and mentor James Stillman. After dining in the silk-draped dining room, they retired for discussion and cigars to the period "French" room. The great men had departed long before we lived there. The paint was peeling and the silk had faded from sunlight. Vanderlip was dead and his children were fighting over their inheritance, but the spirit of the place was still alive.

Above, left: John Cheever with his grandmother Florence Devereaux Liley. *Above, right:* The Cheever house at 123 Winthrop Avenue, which was repossessed by the Wollaston Cooperative Bank in 1933. *Below, left:* John with his beloved older brother Fred. *Below, right:* Frederick Lincoln Cheever with his sons, John and Fred. (Courtesy Jane Cheever Carr)

Above, left: 1931 passport photograph for John Cheever's trip to England and Germany with his brother. *Above, right:* As a private in the army infantry at Fort Gordon, Georgia. *Below:* Walker Evans photograph of the rented room at 633 Hudson Street where John Cheever spent his first months in New York City.

Walker Evans

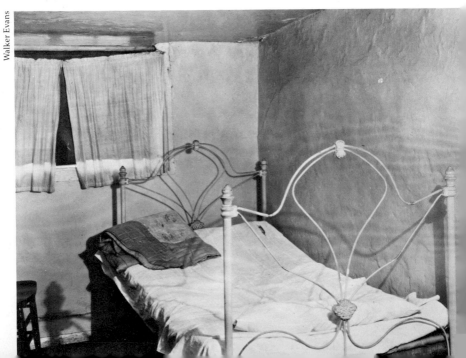

Gustave Lorey

Above: John Cheever (second row, far right) at Yaddo in the summer of 1934, with Muriel Rukeyser (standing at left), James T. Farrell (back row, third from right), Elizabeth Ames (front row center in white dress), et al. (Courtesy Corporation of Yaddo) *Below, left:* The tower of the main house at Yaddo. (Courtesy Corporation of Yaddo) *Below, right:* Mary Winternitz Cheever in 1943.

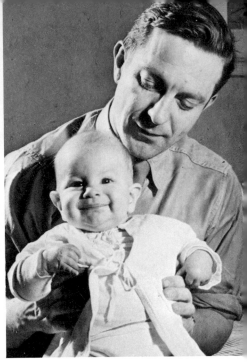

Above, left: John and Mary Cheever at Treetops, New Hampshire, in the early 1940s. *Above, right:* John Cheever with his daughter Susie in 1943. *Below:* Members of the Winternitz, Whitney, and Cheever families at Treetops in 1948: (standing) John Cheever, Mary Cheever holding Ben, Mrs. Pauline Winternitz, and Ethel Whitney; (in front) Dr. Milton Charles Winternitz, Janie Whitney Hotchkiss, Susan Cheever, Steven Whitney, and two cousins.

Above: The author, age five, in the Cheevers' apartment at 400 East 59th Street. *Below, left:* John and Mary Cheever at a suburban picnic in the 1950s after they moved to Westchester. *Below, right:* Cheever in Scarborough in the 1950s.

© Andre Philippon

Above, left: Ben Cheever with his pet mouse Barbara Frietchie at a costume gala on board the *Conte Biancamano. Above, right:* Zinny Schoales on a visit to the Cheevers in Italy. *Below:* The Cheevers and Zinny Schoales in Venice.

Above, left: In the Roman Forum. *Above, right:* Federico Cheever and his nurse, Iole Felici. *Below, left:* The dining room section of the huge salon in the Cheevers' apartment at the Palazzo Doria. *Below, right:* A curtsy during the author's eighth-grade graduation ceremony at the Marymount International School in Rome.

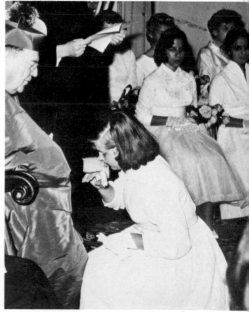

Above: The house in Ossining that the Cheevers bought in 1961. *Below:* John and Mary Cheever at the dinner table in the Ossining house.

© David G.

"Unlike Yaddo or some other big houses, it is more than a ruined rose garden and a string of rooms removed from palaces in France and Italy," my father wrote. "Something has happened here. A plot was outlined in these rooms to rule the world. Presidents and kings were brought here. There is the scene, in the dusk, where Wilson resists their plans and Stillman whispers: 'He is not a great man!' "

From the day our family moved to Beechwood, our lives were inextricably entangled with the lives of the Schoales family on the other side of the estate. To get to the Schoaleses' house I would walk down the lawn past the swimming pool, along a dirt road next to the brook, up a rise toward the farm, past a giant log jutting out of the woods (this was the halfway point), along the edge of the hockey field past the weeping beech whose drooping branches made a natural hide-out, and through an arbor past the rhubarb patch to their kitchen door. I walked that route in all lights and all seasons, alone and with my father, hundreds and hundreds of times. Sarah Schoales, a year older than I, was my best friend. Annie, her little sister, was our sidekick. Dudley, her older brother, was our bitter enemy. Later, he became my first love (unrequited). Virginia, their mother and Frank Vanderlip's daughter, was my father's closest friend, confidante, and drinking companion for more than ten years. Everyone called her Zinny. Big Dudley, their father, a jovial man who had been a star football player at Cornell, thrilled us children by showing how he could vault the living room sofa without spilling a drop of his drink. Dudley was a partner at Morgan Stanley, and he was often away, overseeing his business affairs in the Belgian Congo or in Canada or in Australia. He had parlayed Zinny's Vanderlip money into even more money. It seemed to take up most of his time.

Zinny Schoales was a tall, big-boned woman with short iron-gray hair and enormous blue eyes. Her sister Narcissa had been the family beauty, and Zinny seemed to have the family brains. After she graduated from Barnard, she had worked for Ralph Ingersoll at *PM* in the 1940s, and she had functioned as her father's secretary in the years after he retired from the bank. Her recall was sharp, and she made wonderful stories out of the human comedies she had seen — including those within her own family. Her parents had been horrified when she fell in love with Dudley Schoales, a handsome football star from Cleveland, whose career had consisted principally of sailing from Ithaca, New York, to Ithaca, Greece, in a twenty-five-foot boat with two college friends. She was shipped off to Europe, but she returned a year later and married Dudley just as she had planned.

By the time we moved to Scarborough, Zinny's three children were in school and Dudley was away a lot, and she was rattling around in her barn of a house, running her parents' charities, reading everything, helping anyone she could, managing the Scarborough School from behind the scenes, drinking too much, and passionately following the fortunes of the Brooklyn Dodgers. The house was an eccentric four-story brown shingle structure that she and Dudley had remodeled from the old cow barn at the southern edge of the estate. The center of the house was the three-story living room, which had huge leaded windows facing north and south and dark wood paneling up to about ten feet. The room was painted dark red; on one wall hung a tapestry of Barabbas returning to Cyprus, and on the other walls were Dutch and Italian old-master portraits in heavy gold frames. The furniture was antique but comfortable and shabby, and the sofas and chairs bore unmistakable signs of the family dogs' license to sleep wherever they pleased. You could sink into one of those sofas and look upward into the rich shadows under the roof where the hay had once been stored, or let your eye rest on a painting, or just drift, and centuries of quiet seemed to sift down through the cathedral light.

During the years we lived at Beechwood, my father walked or drove down to Zinny's almost every afternoon and sat and talked with her in the shadows of that room. After we moved to Ossining, he still drove down two or three times a week. They drank and told each other stories. Zinny advised and recounted, my father invented and elaborated. She was an educated woman with the force of culture and wealth behind her, and she certainly helped educate him. I know she taught him something about loyalty when the Vanderlip family accused him of writing about Beechwood in his first novel, *The Wapshot Chronicle*. It was an absurd charge; he had certainly borrowed details and anecdotes, but the book was more his own story than anything else he had written. But it was a serious problem for us. Our tenure at Beechwood was threatened and we had nowhere else to go. Zinny read the book, recognized the family details — many of which she had provided — and understood the situation. She interceded for us with her mother, and after that she and my father were even better friends.

How can I describe the richness and confusion my father brought to all his experience whether he wrote about it or not? He was in flight from a cruel and humiliated father, but the image of the old gent with his simple Yankee ways and his masculine, physical view of the world was in another way everything my father wanted to be. His brother, the same. The dark side of my father's nature was fierce, completely debilitating, and instantly dispelled. In "The Housebreaker of Shady Hill," Johnny Hake is saved from a life of crime — his confidence completely restored — by a few drops of summer rain!

Life for my father was either unbearable or transcendent.

He watched the suburban women's daily migration to the railroad station to drop off their husbands, and sometimes they were a band of angels wearing nightdresses under their coats, and sometimes they were the Furies, nagging and shrill at the wheels of their mortgaged station wagons. He watched the men coming home on the train, and sometimes they were successful gentlemen of good will, and sometimes they were debauched failures fleeing from their own lewd mistakes. Sometimes the lights and music from the suburban parties wafted out of pleasant houses where handsome men and women enjoyed each other's company, and sometimes the parties were grotesque minuets of adulterous golfers and their promiscuous wives. My father noticed too well that the comfortable lives his friends and neighbors had so painstakingly fashioned for themselves were an ineffectual bulwark against the ancient human lusts and expectations that pick up men and women and dash them screaming on the rocks of their own desires. The stories he wrote during those years are so vivid, so alive with detail and pleasure and dread, that for a long time it looked as though that was all anyone would remember of his work.

＊　　＊　　＊

Zinny Schoales died suddenly in 1971; her brother Kelvin and her sister Narcissa had already died of cancer. Her death came more than ten years after my parents moved from Beechwood to Ossining, but in many ways it was the end of a personal era, the end of my family's close connection with Beechwood and the Vanderlip family. She had been eating lunch with Dudley and a friend when she choked and stopped breathing. The funeral service was a few days later in that same red living room where Zinny had held forth so many times in her later years. Her family was there, as were the Vanderlip cousins and uncles and our mutual friends the Kahns and the Swopes and the Boyers. My father read the eulogy he had written, and we all stood on the faded Oriental carpet in the light from the big windows. When the service was finished, there was the harsh, tearing sound of someone sobbing. I don't know who it was, but it seemed as if the house itself was weeping. Afterward we all drove up to the Sleepy Hollow Cemetery and Zinny's ashes were interred in the family vault.

The Schoaleses' house is completely gone now. Where it stood is nothing more than a gap in a line of hemlock trees. The space hardly looks big enough for a house. Through the trees where the back lawn used to be, you can see the white façades of "the Woodland Houses," numbers 23 through 30.

Ten

THE SUBURBS OF New York City in the 1950s were a homogeneous and extended community held together by common interests: children, sports, adultery, and lots of social drinking. Everyone wore costume jewelry — my mother made herself a pair of earrings out of brass screws. It was a time engendered by the winning of the war and destroyed by the upheavals of the 1960s. My parents' generation seemed to believe that thrift, industry, and a modicum of good behavior entitled them to comfortable lives, pleasant neighborhoods, and generally obedient children, with no questions asked. The questions came later.

Scarborough, New York, was typical enough. Everyone had at least two children. In the winter we all skated on the Kahns' pond or on the lake behind the Boyers' or on Crandall's Pond behind the Schoaleses'. In the summer we swam at Beechwood or at the Swopes' or sometimes even in the Hudson River. My mother flirted with the community's businessmen, and my father flirted with their wives. Everyone drank martinis. In the autumn we all played touch football.

My father loved touch. One of the things he taught me was how to wrap my hand around the pigskin with my fingers across the lacing and spin it straight ahead in a forward pass. One Thanksgiving he spent hours laying old tennis tapes on the lawn at Ossining to make it look like a regulation field. Later, when he was older and more famous but less agile, he insisted on playing center. Instead of hiking the ball to the quarterback, he would wait for the count and then run with it, surprising the other team's defensive line and laughing gleefully as he sprinted across the open field and scored a touchdown. It was a measure of his success, I always thought, that no one ever wanted to spoil his pleasure by telling him that his favorite play was against the rules.

My father liked to describe a particularly bullish charge he had made one day during a football game at the Kahns' in the early 1950s. He had careened into the defensive line, knocking over a visitor who had been pressed into the game. It was William Shawn, who had succeeded Harold Ross as the editor of The New Yorker. My father thought that his friend and editor Gus Lobrano should have had the job. Instead, Gus remained fiction editor, and in the 1950s, he turned most of the editing of my father over to William Maxwell, a writer who was also a part-time editor under Lobrano. My father took such delight in telling the story about how he had knocked Mr. Shawn over that I think he must have sensed that his own relationship with The New Yorker was not going to last forever.

In Scarborough, my parents were surrounded by a community of optimistic young couples. There were old friends who had moved to the suburbs at the same time they had, and new ones met at parties or PTA or League of Women Voters meetings: the Schoaleses, the Kahns, the Reimans, the Benjamins, the Engels, and the Swopes, who all lived in Scarborough or Ossining; the Boyers and the Nashes in Croton, where George Biddle and his wife Helene also lived; the Maxwells in Yorktown Heights, and the Ettlingers, and Eddie and Dottie Newhouse across the river. There were cocktail parties and dinner parties and everyone danced the lindy and my father learned to play boogie-woogie on our secondhand baby grand. My mother joined the League of Women Voters, and my father joined the volunteer fire department. Since he was a writer, they made him the fire department secretary. Friends and neighbors often dropped in for a drink and stayed for lunch or dinner. Most people smoked, everyone drank hard liquor. Women didn't have jobs. The Army-McCarthy hearings heightened the liberal community's sense of having something to protect, and Eisenhower was elected president in spite of all their votes for Adlai Stevenson.

Twice a day the tidal flow of cars to and from the railroad station passed our house, and once or twice a week my father joined the commuters on the train, lunched with an editor or an old friend who was still sticking it out in Manhattan, drank too much, sweated it out in the steam room at the old Biltmore Hotel, and took the train home. Ben and I were both enrolled at the Scarborough School, and we were all absorbed into the frantic rounds of car-pooling, parties and community obligations, and flirtations and dreams of prosperity that constituted life in Westchester. My father hated it and he loved it. Sometimes he was too depressed by the banality of his life to work, and other times he was ecstatic. The Hudson Valley light on a spring evening, a child's spontaneous act of generosity, a good story, or the lamplight falling on a pretty woman's hair could redeem the whole world.

On New Year's Eve there was usually a dinner party, then a visit to Beechwood to pay respects at Mrs. Vanderlip's annual gala, and then the costume party at the stables on Teatown Lake in Ossining. The stables were on David Swope's father's estate. David and Sally Swope had become close friends. Their children were near my age, and Sally had the kind of Boston background that always fascinated my father. The New Year's Eve party was the community's major creative effort; the preparations involved dozens of people for months beforehand. Costumes were elaborate and competitive. One year my father pasted on a long gray beard he had bought on Forty-second Street and carried a trident. My mother wreathed herself in flowers and went as Pax. Another year my father wore a helmet and chain mail and my mother's hair got caught in it when they danced. The Schoaleses were always resplendent in outfits from the costume closets at Beechwood.

Each year the dance was planned around a different theme. One year it was heaven and hell. The main room of the stable was decorated to represent hell, and the old tack loft was transformed into cotton-batting heaven. A long slide was built, and the dance committee, dressed as angels, made their entrance by skidding down it in their robes and pasted-on wings. For the party that year my mother spent months working on a huge mural of the seven deadly sins. The canvas was propped up against the piano in the living room while she worked on it, and the daily life of the household went on around its lurid scenes. My father and I practiced the piano — we were both taking lessons from a genteel Croton lady named Levina McClure, who also tutored the Boyers and the Swope and Schoales children. I plinked away at "Flow Gently, Sweet Afton" and "Für Elise," my father played Bach and Chopin and his boogie-woogie. Cassiopeia, our black Labrador puppy, chewed the fiery edges of the mural. Cassie was the first of three dogs we got from litters bred by Phil Boyer. Phil and Mimi and their three children lived in a big house in Croton. Phil was in advertising, but he was principally a gentleman — tall, aristocratic, and A.D. at Harvard. Phil went hunting with his dogs and played wonderful tennis and took us up to the Harvard-Yale game in his vintage brown Plymouth that he had named Apple Pan Dowdy. My father loved him. His other close friend in the community was Arthur Spear, a transplanted Yankee gentleman whose father had been a painter of the Boston school. Arthur and my father went to services together at All Saints Church, and skated together at the Boyers', and walked their black Labradors together, and played fierce backgammon for pennies. Arthur and his wife Stella had three daughters. When my father was writing *The Wapshot Chronicle*, he used Arthur's grandfather Hezekiah Prince's journals, as well as his own father's journals, as models for Leander Wapshot's.

A few years after we moved to Scarborough, Pepperell transferred my father's brother Fred to a job in New York City. Fred and Iris bought a substantial Tudor-style house, with its own lawns and woods, in Scarborough, just across Route 9 and down Marlborough Road from our small rented house. They moved in and enrolled their two youngest children, Sue and Nanny, in local schools (Jane and their son David were already away at boarding school). I don't remember much about the year or two they lived there before moving on to Westport; my father kept to himself his feelings about his brother's proximity. Although they lived half a mile away, we didn't see them very often. I remember Uncle Fred coming into my room in the house at Scarborough once after bedtime to tell me a joke that I found hilarious — and I remember my parents' displeasure. At Christmas, my aunt Iris made colored lollipops from molds, in the shapes of trees and hands and roosters, and sometimes on a summer evening I would walk down to their house for a game of badminton on the lawn with my cousins.

In warm weather the Hudson Valley landscape seemed to soften and sweeten, to bloom and then to rot. Summer nights at Beechwood were heavy with the fragrance of honeysuckle and roses, the animal musks of the farm, and the sweetness of new-mown grass. We escaped the steamy air by diving into the icy water of the swimming pool.

Soon after his brother moved away, my father wrote, describing one of those summer nights, "In the stillness the throbbing of a ship's motor sounded clearly from the river. It was some big craft — a tanker or freighter riding high. The sound of the screw deepened as she passed and then slacked off as she went upriver. Overhead a plane crossed with all her gaudy landing lights still burning, she seemed to proceed very slowly below the large stars. The tree frogs sang loudly; soon will come the winter cold. It was the hottest night of the year. At my back I heard some rats in the cistern. In the little skin of light on the water I saw bats hunting. For a second everything that was familiar and pleasant seemed ugly. In the woods a cat began to howl like a demented child. The water smelled stagnant. I went in, swam, climbed out and walked back over the grass. Religious things, superstitious things, what Veblen calls the devoutness of the delinquent — whatever it was I seemed to step into a pleasant atmosphere of goodness, a turning in the path that seemed to state clearly; Joy to the world, lasting Joy. Awoke at two; smoked on the stones; still the loud noise of tree frogs. The cat drifted home. Many stars."

✳   ✳   ✳

I had imagined my father dying many times. I had imagined the telephone call and the impersonal voice of the doctor or the police officer at the other end of the line. I had imagined hearing it over the car radio, or reading it in a telegram slipped under the door of some European hotel. My father was often sick in the 1960s and 1970s, and each time he went into the hospital the possibility of his death hung over us. With my father, even the smallest operation always seemed critical. As he got older and drank more and more, his visits to the hospital became even more threatening.

Once, late at night when my brother Fred and I were leaving the parking lot of the local hospital — Phelps Memorial Hospital in North Tarrytown — we stole the No Parking sign near the emergency exit and stashed it in the back of the car. It was a warm night in 1973, and inside the hospital my father was lying in a drugged stupor after his first major heart attack. We had taken turns sitting at his bedside through three days of delirium tremens. Fred and I were punchy and exhausted that night, but there's nothing so bad that my family can't make a joke out of it. When he dies, we said to each other, we'll steal the One Way sign.

But he didn't die that time, and the No Parking sign rusted against the woodpile at the end of the driveway all during his recovery and his relapse and the final crisis and his recovery after that.

In December of 1981, when my father was sixty-nine, we found out that he had terminal cancer. I went out to Ossining to visit him as often as I could then, and we used to sit around and joke and talk about the past.

"There's a story about Nar," he said one day, referring to Zinny Schoales's sister Narcissa. I was sitting on the end of his bed. "I never wanted to believe it, because I didn't like her."

I picked at the bedspread and kept my head down. I knew the story. "She never liked us either," he said. "We never were invited to her parties. But when she found out that her cancer was terminal, she asked herself what she was best at. She was a great hostess. She gave a dazzling sit-down dinner for forty. Then she drove up to their house in Connecticut and took the pills."

Later, when his disease had been diagnosed as renal cancer and famous oncologists had been called in for the treatment, I took a taxi down to Sixty-eighth Street to wait with him while they made up the room he had during the first of his two stays at Memorial Hospital. My father always dressed up for the hospital in a tweed suit and silk bow tie, his blue cashmere coat, gloves, his cane, and even a felt hat. I found him sitting in the waiting room on the eleventh floor, on one of a set of molded green plastic chairs. I sat next to him on a plastic wicker sofa with bright-green cushions. Some demented mind had decorated this way station between life and death to resemble a summer arbor, with everything trimmed in green plastic and phony lattice-work painted on the walls. At first my father was glad to be at Memorial, where he thought they might know how to save him. Later he said it was a charnel house. At one end of the waiting room a color television was blaring a soap opera. We tried to talk to each other over the sound.

"I saved up the pills I had," my father said. "I saved them until I had enough." The television played the theme from *General Hospital*. Luke appeared on the screen, arguing with a man in a white lab coat.

"Let me turn that off," I said. We were alone in the waiting room. I played with the television set's on/off button, but instead of switching off, the picture swayed and faded to a deep, out-of-focus purple. I turned off the volume.

"I put the pills I had saved in the drawer of my bedside table," my father said. Out the window I could see some white brick buildings, and beyond them the turbulent currents of the East River boiling against its banks. A nurse came in to watch the television. She sat down for a moment and then got up and fiddled with the dials. The sound came up, but the picture did not refocus. She left the room.

"I kept thinking about them," my father said. "Then one day when I was with Don Ettlinger I mentioned it to him. Telling someone made it seem less important."

Two interns came into the room smoking cigarettes, and one of them gave the television an angry thump on its side. Nothing changed. The characters continued their wavy purple progress through the day's inexorable plot.

"No *General Hospital* today," one of the interns said.

"Shit," the other one said.

"After that," my father said, "I took them out of the bedside table and put them back in the medicine cabinet."

When his room was ready, we walked down the hall together and I unpacked his suitcase and hung his bathrobe in the narrow closet. From his bed he could see the spire of the Chrysler Building, and the lacy minarets of the Queensboro Bridge where we used to take our afternoon walks.

❋   ❋   ❋

A black and white piece of Japanese calligraphy in a gold frame hangs on the wall of the master bedroom at the house in Ossining. It's a quotation from the writer Kawabata, who killed himself in 1972.

"Do you know what that says?" my father asked me, as he lay there the Christmas before he died. I shook my head. Bright scraps of ribbon and paper from the Christmas presents littered the floor. My father looked up from the pillows. "Because you cannot see him, God is everywhere."

Eleven

By THE TIME MY FATHER was forty years old, he had been trying to write a novel for almost twenty years. Without a novel, there could be no solid literary reputation. A few years after he came to New York, he showed Malcolm Cowley a draft of a novel, and Cowley discouraged him. It was too obviously based on the Hemingway story "Cross-Country Snow," Cowley wrote later: "It would have been the equivalent of Jackson Pollock's attempts to copy the Sistine Chapel." My father threw the novel away.

His letters to my mother before their marriage are often about his work on another novel, "The Holly Tree." (One of the largest holly trees in New England grew outside his aunt Mary Thompson's house in Hanover.) The letters were filled with self-flagellation: he wasn't working hard enough, the narrative was weak, he would never finish it. He had taken a small advance from Simon & Schuster, and when he finally gave up, he paid them back.

By the early 1950s he had published almost a hundred stories, more than seventy of them in *The New Yorker*, where he had been appearing regularly since 1935. His six

"Town House" stories (about three families living together in an Upper East Side town house) had been produced as a play at the National Theatre, directed by George S. Kaufman. He had won the Benjamin Franklin Short Story Award and been included in four of the O. Henry *Prize Stories* collections. But still no novel. He started work on a novel again in the 1950s, and by 1954, when he was forty-two, he had finished a draft of the first section of *The Wapshot Chronicle*, for which he had received a $2500 advance from Random House. The book was a distillation of his earlier ideas, and based on his boyhood experience. It's a novel about two brothers growing up in a small town on the South Shore, and about their father, the "old gent," a noble man humiliated by an eccentric and overbearing wife.

We were living in the little house at Beechwood then, and I remember the charged air in the family as the novel began to take shape. The house had two bedrooms and a bathroom upstairs and two small bedrooms with an adjoining bathroom off the living room. One of the downstairs bedrooms was mine, and the other was, intermittently, my father's workroom. He also worked upstairs in the master bedroom, down the hill in a rented office above the Scarborough railroad station, and in various borrowed rooms and offices in the neighborhood. When my parents moved to their house in Ossining, my father shuttled his work in progress back and forth between the maid's room behind the kitchen and the upstairs bedrooms vacated by children away at school or college. He also rented an office above a real estate office in Ossining, and a room at the back of the Swopes' house on Hawkes Avenue. Once, when we were all home from school for the summer, he pitched a tent on the lawn behind the house and took his aluminum folding table, his ream of cheap paper, and his Olivetti portable out there to work. "It's quite dark but for a soft green light, the color of artificial lime drink," he wrote his editor William Maxwell. "At night everything gets wet."

He was a writer who refused to sentimentalize his profession, preferring to work in temporary quarters and on a portable typewriter. It was almost as if he was afraid that a study with book-lined walls and neatly filed papers and his own oeuvre bound in leather would be too much of a burden for his talent. He was scornful of other people's well-appointed studies and often noted, with some justification, that the elegance of their surroundings did not seem to help their writing.

As *The Wapshot Chronicle* came to life, the center of the family seemed to shift down and eastward to where my father was working that year. He was in the downstairs guest room typing most of the day and sometimes at night. When people came to visit, instead of heading for the kitchen, or plumping themselves down on the sofa, they knocked on the door of the guest room. No one was ever particularly respectful of my father's working hours, and he never had a strict writing schedule. He rarely seemed irritated when he was interrupted, and he was always ready to welcome a guest or answer the telephone or retrieve a lost hamster.

But *writing* the novel turned out to be just the beginning of my father's troubles with getting *The Wapshot Chronicle* published. He never talked much about his struggles to get the book written, but he told the stories about his problems getting it published again and again. When he thought he had finished enough of the novel to show an editor, he took the train to New York City and delivered it. Weeks went by. Then, my father said, the editor summoned him to his office and turned the novel down. When my father, distraught, mentioned that he didn't see how he could pay the advance back, the editor remarked that Random House had a life insurance policy written into the book contract. Perhaps it was a flat joke, or an aside. Who knows what the editor really said; but the effect of his words was devastating. My father's self-esteem was always fragile, and this was an unusually vulnerable moment. He thought the editor was suggesting that he commit suicide. He took the manuscript off the editor's desk, walked out of the Random House offices, and caught the early train home to Scarborough.

Years later, when I was dealing with editors myself, he told me another version of the novel's fate at Random House. According to this story, a junior editor had been assigned to tell him what changes were needed to make the book acceptable. They were extensive. My father didn't say anything as the editor obtusely slashed away at page after page. He nodded politely. When she was finished, he took the manuscript off her desk, thanked her, and left the publishing house for good. It wasn't that my father rejected all editing. He was certainly grateful for the guidance Malcolm Cowley gave him, and he took hundreds of suggestions for changes and revisions from Gus Lobrano and Bill Maxwell. Still, he loved to quote the axiom, "Trust your editor, and you'll sleep on straw."

Flat broke, in debt for the advance, uncertain about the future of his novel, my father packed us all up and drove us to Nantucket, where he had rented the Swopes' house for the month of July.

"I see a world of monsters and beasts; my grasp on creative and wholesome things is gone. To justify this I think of the violence of the past; an ugly house and exacerbating loneliness," he wrote in his journal before we left. "How far I have come, I think, but I do not seem to have come far at all. I am haunted by some morbid conception of beauty-cum-death for which I am prepared to destroy myself. And so I think that life is a contest, that the forces of good and evil are strenuous and apparent, and that while my self-doubt is profound, nearly absolute, the only thing I have to proceed on is an invisible thread. So I proceed on this."

We stopped for the night at a motel in Woods Hole, and during the hours before dawn, my father thought he heard me calling for him. Disoriented and half asleep, he stumbled out of his room and into another. Staring at the faces of two startled strangers, he wondered for a moment how his two children had grown so old and so homely.

The Swopes' house is in Wauwinet, on a bluff with a commanding view of Nantucket's upper harbor and the spit of sand called Coatue and the sea beyond that. My father's workroom was at the front of the house, and from the window he could see the harbor, the gray shingle pile of the old Wauwinet House down the beach, and the cluster of ramshackle cottages that was Wauwinet in those days before the whole world descended on the seashore. One day my father was looking out the window when he saw a gleaming sailing yacht tacking in past Polpis and along Coatue to the harbor. The little ketch was so trim and so neatly handled that by the time it turned onto a broad reach in front of the Wauwinet House, a few people had come down to watch, and others were at their windows. The graceful boat anchored, and a dinghy was lowered from the polished deck. A man in white flannels and a double-breasted blazer stepped into it and was rowed to shore. By the time he threw his leg over the gunwale onto the sand, a small crowd had gathered.

"I'm looking for John Cheever," the man said in the unmistakable accent of the literate aristocrat. It was Simon Michael Bessie, a senior editor at Harper & Brothers, and he had come to buy *The Wapshot Chronicle*.

Mike Bessie doesn't remember it quite that way. In his version of the story, he and my father met at a lunch party in Chappaqua, a town near Scarborough. (Later, he knew my parents on Nantucket, where he summered with his wife, Connie.) Soon after that, my father wrote him a note, hinting at his predicament with Random House and inviting him to buy the unfinished novel for the price of the advance. Even this far down on his luck, my father had conditions to make. The novel might never be finished, he warned Bessie, and if Harper wanted to buy it they could only do so if no one there ever asked how the book was going.

Bessie responded immediately. "I called him up and said, 'Where do I send the check?' " he remembers. When I told Mike Bessie my father's version of their meeting, he laughed with pleasure and astonishment. He had never sailed anything but a thirteen-foot Rainbow; furthermore, the water off Polpis is too shallow for a yacht of any size to clear the shoals and make it into Wauwinet harbor.

But accuracy is irrelevant here, as it is in many of my father's stories about his life. His and Mike Bessie's are two different stories, but in a way they are the same story — a story about a proud and talented writer being rescued from humiliation and poverty by a man who had enough faith in him to take a chance; a story about courage in the face of defeat, and its eventual magic rewards. A suburban lunch party was an inadequate setting for the sense of gratitude, exoneration, and vindication that my father must have felt when he got the check from Harper & Brothers and paid Random House back. Bessie's arrival on the scene was a triumphal entry, a triumphal rescue, and my father told the story accordingly.

Harper & Brothers published *The Wapshot Chronicle* in the winter of 1957. The novel sold well, it was bought by the Book-of-the-Month Club, the reviews were favorable, and a year later it won the National Book Award. Soon afterward my father was elected to the National Institute of Arts and Letters, and he immediately composed a ditty for the occasion: "Root tee toot, ahhh root tee toot, oh we're the boys from the Institute. Oh we're not rough and we're not tough, we're *cul*tivated and that's enough."

By that time, though, we had taken the advance for the finished book — the first extra money my father had ever had — and boarded the Italian Line's *Conte Biancamano*, bound for Naples via Lisbon, Casablanca, Gibraltar, Barcelona, Cannes, Palermo, and Genoa.

A year in Italy! What a magical idea it seemed as we spread the maps of the exotic boot-shaped peninsula on the floor of the living room and spent hours listening to Berlitz living-language records. "Buon giorno, Signora." "Buona sera, Signora." "Per favore." "Per piacere." "Grazie tante." My father needed a change. I craved adventure. Standing with him on the bridge of the ocean liner as we moved out of the slip and down the Hudson past the Statue of Liberty, I thought that we were ready for anything.

Another family might have hesitated. I was thirteen, my brother Ben was eight, and my mother was four months pregnant. None of us spoke any Italian. No arrangements had been made for our arrival in Rome. We did not know where we would live, where Ben and I would go to school for the year that had already begun, or what my mother's obstetrical situation would be. But who cared? Those things were not important at all! We were off.

I'm not sure how my parents decided on Italy. In the early 1950s, my father had developed a passion for Italian opera, and we listened to *Don Giovanni*, *La Traviata*, and *Tosca* over and over again on the tinny-sounding Victrola in the Scarborough living room. His friends Eleanor Clark and her husband Robert Penn Warren may have urged them to go. But I suspect it was more a process of elimination. My father had been to Germany with his brother Fred when he was younger, and he spoke some German. So my mother didn't want to go there. My mother had gone to school in Switzerland for two years, and she had spent a summer bicycling through France with a friend from Sarah Lawrence. It had been one of the happiest summers of her life, she said, and she spoke passable French of which she was extremely proud. Naturally my father didn't want to go there. Not only did he not want to live in France, he never even visited France. He went to London and Rome, Moscow and Leningrad, Bucharest and Sofia, Frankfurt and Amsterdam — but he never saw Paris. When I asked him about this once, he said that it was because the other men in E Company had been killed in France. I don't think so. I think my mother's passion for France and the French kept him away — even in the 1970s when my second husband and I went to live there.

The *Conte Biancamano* was a small, elegant liner that had once ferried the F. Scott Fitzgeralds to Italy. We stopped at every port, and between Genoa and Palermo we were called up on deck so that we children could get a close look at Monte Cristo, a mysterious, cavernous mountaintop jutting straight out of the deep blue offshore Mediterranean. Waves whipped up against its precipitous cliffs, and as we watched from the rail we could almost hear the sound of Edmond Dantès' picks as he dug for the treasure spoken of by the dying abbé in the dungeons of the Château D'If.

In Palermo we learned that Europe was on the verge of war. We had spent the afternoon with the mosaics at Monreale, where God is a glittery figure who looks like a rich old man, and we were sipping *aranciatas* at a sidewalk café, when a gang of newsboys came tearing down the street, calling out the news of a third world war and waving tabloids with blood-red headlines. Egypt had moved to nationalize the Suez Canal. In Rome the news seemed even more ominous. France and England were at war with Egypt. Israeli troops were occupying the Sinai. We checked into La Residenza, a pleasantly seedy literary *pensione* on the Via Emilia below the Villa Borghese gardens. Our family had two rooms; one for my parents, and one for me and Ben and Ben's pet mouse, Barbara Frietchie. My brother loved mice. I had been through the predictable hamster and white-rat phases of early childhood, but this was nothing like Ben's passion. When we left Scarborough for Italy, we left the dog, Cassiopeia, behind with our subtenants. There was no question of leaving Barbara Frietchie. A large mouse with a long white body and tiny pink feet, she had been Ben's constant companion and principal comfort on the trip, especially when she was smuggled through Italian customs peeking out of the pocket of my mother's maternity coat.

Barbara had been named for the gallant Yankee woman in John Greenleaf Whittier's poem about Stonewall Jackson's entry into Fredericktown. The day we got her was the day I finished memorizing the poem's verses for our Sunday recitation. Every Sunday after dinner, we each recited a poem for the rest of the family. It began with sonnets and short narrative verse, Shakespeare and Tennyson, but soon we were spending whole weekends in competitive feats of memory. My father memorized Dylan Thomas's "Fern Hill," my mother countered with Keats's "Ode to a Nightingale," I did "Barbara Frietchie," my father did "The Charge of the

Light Brigade," and so forth. Ben, who was eight, stayed with shorter poems. (My father gave one of his least-successful writing assignments around this time, when he asked his class at Barnard to memorize "Fern Hill." He had learned something from doing this, he reasoned, and they would too. They refused. His negative feelings about teaching were reinforced. Then, a week later, three of his best students appeared at his office door to recite the poem in perfect unison.)

In the poem, Barbara Frietchie's problem is General Jackson. But Barbara Frietchie the mouse had a different problem: she smelled. Every day we spent in the *pensione*, she smelled worse. Ben cleaned her cage, but fresh cedar chips didn't seem to make any difference. Each time she scrabbled to the bars or took a turn on her wheel, the smell would waft chokingly across our room in spite of the open windows. Baby sitters eagerly took us out for walks rather than stay there. The smell persisted, pungent and revolting. One night after Ben and I had gone down to dinner, my father took a bottle of my mother's perfume — Ma Griffe, as it happened — and sprayed Barbara and her cage. The next day she was dead.

We found her there at the end of the afternoon, stiff and lifeless in her cage, and we were inconsolable. My mother emptied a shoe box and made an elaborate coffin. My father left the *pensione* and his weeping children carrying the coffin under his arm in the cold twilight, having promised to perform a royal burial and lay Barbara next to Pauline Bonaparte in the Villa Borghese gardens up the street. Wandering the alleys of a foreign city in the autumn night, carrying a dead mouse in a shoe box, my father may have had second thoughts about our great adventure. The rest of us did. We were lonely, homesick, and disoriented. I yearned for the school and friends I had so lately fled.

"We have been here a little over a week now, but with the exception of my first days in the infantry I have never felt time to be so distorted," my father wrote home to Bill Maxwell. "I look at four and five apartments a day, and Mary visits schools. . . . The whole expedition from the moment we boarded the boat has meant a complete reconstruction of my machinery and I guess my biliousness about the American Romans can be charged to this. They talk gaily about the certainty of war and with their Roman clothes and jewelry and their knowledge of good, small restaurants, they seem to be fulfilling ambitions that must have been formed in the kitchens and backyards of small and lonely American towns. The war news is difficult to assess because I can't read Italian and because the press here is irresponsible. Dusk is a great tumult of traffic noises, lovely clouds, noisy crowds, and scare headlines. There was one evening, after a cocktail party, when I thought of taking the family home. There are many evacuees from Cairo in the Pension here."

Eventually I went to Marymount International School and Ben to the Overseas School, and my father found a dazzlingly grand and gloomy apartment on the fourth floor of the Palazzo Doria, just off the Piazza Venezia. The center of the apartment was a vast salon divided into three sections by screens: the dining room (portrait, sideboard, Empire table, and chairs); the reading room (huge satin armchairs, marble coffee table, phony Titian in heavy gold frame); and the living room (fireplace, smaller chairs and end tables, Victorian scroll sofa). The salon and the huge master bedroom took up most of the living space. There were cherubs and garlands carved into plaster lozenges in the ceilings, and black and white marble floors. In the back of the apartment a long unlit hall led to two cramped bedrooms, a tiny bathroom, and a kitchen with no refrigerator. My father loved the apartment, and he was fascinated by our landlady, the Principessa Doria, and her stories about escaping from the Nazis out the back door of the apartment with her father the Prince. In the typically Roman ceremony of paying the rent and taking the key from the Principessa, he had forgotten to ask about the kitchen. When my mother saw that tiny back room with its dingy window and creaking food cupboards, she burst into tears.

"There has been too much," my father wrote Maxwell. "Arabs, cathedrals, ship-board friends, games of musical chairs in black tie, the coast of Spain off Tarragona, the death of Benjamin's white mouse, the war, hurdy-gurdies, white truffles with scrambled eggs as a side dish, cocktail parties, Castel Sant'Angelo, gale winds and high seas, the sweetness of the children, real estate agents and the news in the *London Times*. I don't think I can make sense until we are settled."

Rome was never a good place for my father to work, and many of his letters to Maxwell are apologetic. He tried setting up his typewriter on the ornate cornices of the dining room table, under the portrait of the Doria Cardinal, but his ideas seemed to get lost between the top of his head and the distant, garland-encrusted ceiling. He tried working in a corner of the master bedroom looking out over the wrought-iron balcony and the Palazzo Venezia. He tried working in our rooms while we were at school. At first he had to cope with our homesickness and his own disorientation, later there were the final months of my mother's pregnancy, and after that the new baby.

It was a rainy autumn with occasional golden days, and Rome in the 1950s had not recovered from the war. There were fewer cars than motorbikes and bicycles, beggars were on every street corner and in front of every church, and

everyone remembered that life had been better under Musso-
lini. The streets were dirty, the great ruins and monuments
unlit and unguarded. It was still possible to wander anywhere in the Forum, or to leave the Capitoline with frag-
ments of ancient marble in your pockets. The churches hung
mattresses in their doorways to keep out the cold.

I spent hours turning the hand-crank portable Victrola,
which was my only source of music, playing and replaying
my favorite Elvis Presley forty-five, "I Was the One" /
"Heartbreak Hotel." "Oh I'm so lonely baby, I been so lonely,
I been so lonely I could die . . ." I would croon, snatching
a moment's sad pleasure before I had to recrank the little
machine for the flip side. I imagined my friends back home
in Scarborough, and the wonderful times they must be
having now that rock 'n' roll was born.

On the street corner of the Via del Plebiscito and the
Piazza del Gesù, where I waited for the school bus with my
father every morning, there was usually a cold wind that
whipped through my blue serge blazer and lifted the skirts
of the French teacher who stood there with us. The square
is dominated by the stone building that houses the principal
Jesuit church in Rome, and my father loved to horrify the
French teacher with his favorite story about how the wind
and the Devil were walking down the Via del Plebiscito, just
as we were, when they reached the corner of the Piazza del
Gesù. "Wait for me a minute while I go in here," the Devil
said to the wind, and he disappeared through the doors of
the Jesuit church. They say that the Piazza del Gesù is the
windiest square in Rome.

In the first term I had failed two subjects in school, and
Ben was sick with the flu. My mother's obstetrician diagnosed her weight gain as toxemia and put her on a diet of
spinach and lemon juice, adding some diuretic pills.

Twelve

SOMETIME DURING THAT RAINY Roman autumn, my mother made an appointment to interview a woman named Iole Felici for the position of housekeeper and baby nurse. There had been other interviews, all discouraging. By then we spoke some Italian, but there was still a frustrating language and culture barrier when it came to talking about something as complicated and crucial as baby care. With Iole there was no language barrier — there wasn't even an interview. She arrived, assessed the situation, and took over. A short, dark woman with energy to burn, she shooed my mother out of the kitchen, reorganized the household, and even hired another maid to do the heavy work. Iole's salary was thirty-five cents an hour. She came from Capranica *sopra* Viterbo, but she called herself a Roman. She had been engaged for ten years to a man from Capranica who felt that he couldn't marry her until his mother died. In the meantime, she had us. She let me know what she thought of my grades— and with my intelligence! And she lectured my father when he carried the groceries or dressed too casually. He would make a *bruta figura*, she said. We were her family, and we had better shape up. She fed us and laundered our clothes and bullied us into better behavior, and when my mother was delivered of a baby boy at the Salvador Mundi hospital on March 9, she took over his care almost completely. He was the prince of the household, and my father used to joke that if my mother wanted to see her baby, Iole would tell her that he was busy, he had *cosa da fare*, things to do, and he would fit her in when he could.

Iole's energy revitalized our adventure. Everything improved. The British and the French backed down, Anthony Eden's government fell, Egypt kept the Suez, and there was no more talk of war. I got A's instead of F's and my father came shyly into my room one day to give me a 10,000-lira note and say how proud he was. Ben's health improved and we acquired a pair of black and white spotted dancing mice named Giuseppe and Pepe Le Moco who whirled around each other in a mousy minuet.

My father had decided to name his third child after his father, Frederick Lincoln Cheever. But when he went to have the birth registered, the certificate couldn't be made out in that name because there is no *k* in the Italian alphabet. This evidence of the distance we had traveled pleased him, I think, and as a result of it my brother's legal name is Federico. When he was a baby, Iole called him *picci*, which means "little one" in Italian, and so we all called him Picci. He had had enough of that by the time he was eight, and now everyone calls him Fred.

My father understood the importance of other languages and other cultures. Although he spoke minimal French, he always called the French classics by their original names: *Les Faux-Monnayeurs*, *La Chartreuse de Parme*, *Le Rouge et le Noir*. In his last years — a time when he was so well respected that a lot of people assumed he spoke two or three languages — he began dropping French words into his con-

versation. When he was sent his own books in French trans-
lations, he kept them on the desk or his bedside table. With
Italian, he was even worse. He spoke a stilted, conversational
Italian, but he used it at every opportunity, and he even
insisted on re-Italianizing all Americanized Italian words or
names. (He always insisted on calling my editor Nan Talese
"Nan Talayzee," for instance.)

"Che cosa di buona oggi?" he would ask any dark-haired
waiter, whether he was at the Four Seasons or the Highland
diner on Route 9 in Ossining. They were always very polite.

The funniest example of his struggle with Italian happened when we had been in Rome about six months. Vittoria, the young country girl Iole had hired, used to bring
my parents breakfast in bed, and she always peeled the
boiled eggs. My father liked to eat his boiled egg out of
the shell, first slicing off the top with a sharp knife. He
studied the dictionary carefully, finding the word for egg,
the word for kitchen, and the word for peel. In the morning,
when Vittoria appeared, he cleared his throat and carefully
asked her not to peel the eggs in the kitchen. Vittoria
shrieked, blushed, and rushed from the room in tears. What
my father had said was, "Do not undress in the kitchen,
you egg." The fact that Vittoria had been changing her
clothes in the kitchen didn't help. Iole stepped in and the
incident was smoothed over.

In June, I graduated with the Marymount eighth grade
in a formal ceremony involving a curtsy to the ground and
a bow over the bishop's ring, swinging my masses of ring-
lets, which had been created by Iole with rags and hairpins.
My father loved ritual, and he often produced the photograph of my curly head bent over the chubby fingers of
God's anointed. For me, it had been a narrow escape. The
pressure to convert to Catholicism was significant at Marymount, and Rome was a fertile environment. Instead I

became a confirmed Episcopalian in a damp winter ceremony at St. Paul's, the American church on the Via Nazionale. I still wavered, however, and the mother superior assured me it was not too late. If my calling was great enough, I could become a nun. Heaven and hell were much on my mind. And if adolescence was life, I thought, I wouldn't mind trading it for a guarantee of heaven. I had also come to love my Marymount teachers, and I wanted to be like them. Once, in the twilight on the terrace of a *pensione* where we were staying in Fiesole, on the hill above Florence, I mentioned these desires to my father. The sun was setting in an orange blaze behind the Duomo. "That would break my heart," he said.

But all this time my father was feasting on Italy. Even when he was miserable, he loved it. He loved the exotic formality of the Italian manners and the extravagance of the Italian soul: Iole, who wouldn't think of going shopping without wearing her highest heels and her squirrel-paw fur jacket; the Principessa Doria, who told him stories about how she and her brother had dyed their fair hair and spent the war years hiding in the slums of Trastevere; the flapping and chattering maidservants, who walked ahead of us on their way to work when we went to the school-bus corner. He loved the gloom of the vaulted ceilings at Santa Maria in Aracoeli, the *palazzo* doors so huge that smaller doors had been cut into them for people, the apricot and orange stuccos, and the delicious light below the Gianicolo in the evening; all reached out to him. He studied Roman history and read everything he could find on Italian heroes, battles, and politics, from Hannibal to Garibaldi and the *Risorgimento*. (In "The Country Husband," one of his famous images, which is often taken to be surreal — "It is a night where kings in golden suits ride elephants over the mountains" — was in fact based on a description of Hannibal, the Carthaginian general who invaded Rome by bringing elephants over the Alps with his troops. He wore golden armor.) My father took hundreds of walks in Rome, down the Via del Corso and over to the Pantheon and through the Forum and down the Via del Piè di Marmo with its pedal fragment of an ancient statue, or across the Piazza del Gesù and into the labyrinth of streets near the Palazzo Farnese and the Piazza Navona. He kept going back to Italy for the rest of his life.

There's a cultural axis between Boston and Rome, as there was between London and Florence in the nineteenth century. The fabulous scale of the Roman architecture and the ancient basilicas and forums are amazing to men who have been raised under the low ceilings and gabled spaces of New England houses. There the light is spare and wintry. In Rome it is orange and peach-colored as it reflects off vast, ornamented façades. I was writing a book report about Nathaniel Hawthorne that spring for my teacher at Marymount, and my father talked to me about what the excesses of Rome must have meant to the author of *The Scarlet Letter*. In Massachusetts, they had abhorred all ornament and luxury, he explained. Even buttons were useless and sinful adornments, modesty was so valued that *piano* legs were never mentioned, and underwear was hung out on the clothesline concealed in special pillowcases. In Rome, everything is massive, opulent, decorated to the limit. (We were sitting in the satin chairs, under the cherub-encrusted ceiling, next to the marble coffee table.) Look around you, he said. Look at these chairs, the frame on that Titian, the size of this room! It must have taken more than that, but I remember the connections he made between Rome and New England as one of my first inklings that literature might apply to me. Books, even old-fashioned books, might be about my life and the lives of people I knew, although they

were ostensibly about those who were long ago and far
away.

In Rome I turned thirteen, and our talks about Hawthorne
were the beginning of the intense, often uncomfortable
intellectual discussions I had with my father for the rest of
his life. I began to read obsessively — all of Hawthorne,
all of Balzac, all of Nancy Drew. I rewrote my book report,
pointing out in one paragraph that Lizzie Borden was the
Beatrice Cenci of Fall River, Massachusetts. The teachers
were alarmed; my father was delighted. English books were
scarce in Rome, and it was a big treat for me when he took
the bus to the Red Lion Bookshop on the Via del Babuino
and came home with a package. If it was a novel by Wilkie
Collins or Alexandre Dumas, I was inevitably stricken with
a mysterious illness the next morning. But the minute my
mother pronounced me too sick to go to school, I would
recover enough to sit up and grope for the book with my
weakened hands. My father was delighted; the teachers
were alarmed.

We talked about everything I read. We took long walks
and talked. On Sunday mornings we went to early communion at St. Paul's to hear Thomas Cranmer's exquisite
service from the Book of Common Prayer. We both knew
it by heart, and we looked on members of the congregation
who had to refer to the prayer book during the service with
distinctly unchristian contempt. Afterward we had bacon
and fried eggs in the American Bar on the Via Nazionale
and walked home.

After our return from Italy, we talked in the living room
of the house in Scarborough night after night, so that I was
groggy in the morning and bored with school. How could
my teachers compete with my father's stories, his discussions
of books and language? When I did perk up in the classroom,
it was usually to challenge something the teacher had said.

When we moved from Beechwood, my father and I had our talks in the dining room of the house in Ossining, with my father sitting in the yellow wing chair his mother had given my parents when they married. In the summer we talked sitting on chairs or on the steps of the front porch; and when he got sick we talked in my old bedroom, where he slept for the last years of his life, and in private rooms at Memorial Hospital and Mount Kisco Hospital, and, during the final months of his life, in the master bedroom at Ossining.

❋   ❋   ❋

In July of our Italian summer we drove up the coast to a village on the Monte Argentario called Port'Ercole. Now it's a chic international resort with harborside condominiums and first-class hotels. Then it was a dilapidated group of fishermen's houses dominated by a sardine-canning factory. We stayed in the Rocca, a vast and crumbling fortress that overlooked the harbor and the Mediterranean. It was the most beautiful place any of us had ever seen. Since then the Rocca has become a deluxe hotel and the summer residence of princesses and jewelry designers, but in 1957 conditions there were as primitive as they had been when it was built by Francis I for his soldiers. All water was drawn by bucket from an icy well, we slept in abandoned doorless and windowless barracks on lumpy straw mattresses, and the slimy beetles called *maialini di San Antonio* (St. Anthony's little pigs) were everywhere. But the days were filled with adventures and fabulous vistas of the sea. Under the old walls there were passageways and caverns that we explored by candlelight, and everyone knew treasure was buried somewhere in the dusty grass of the moat. There were the etched lines of the ruined foundations against the summer sky and, from the guard towers, the view of the Mediterranean — blue and then green and then, farther out, purple, until it reached the hazy pastel of the horizon over Corsica. The fortress was owned by the elusive "Signorina," a stooped old woman in black who lived on the other side of the parade ground near the well. We were at the Rocca through the generosity of Eleanor Clark (the author of *Rome and a Villa*) and Robert Penn Warren. Eleanor had befriended the Signorina and her servant Ernesta during her Italian travels, and she had spent a lot of time at the Rocca even during the war.

It took about four weeks for the simmering hatred between Ernesta, the ensconced power, and our Iole to explode. I only remember that it was a fight over some figs we had picked on the battlements. Ernesta said they were her figs. The two women started toward each other in the lower courtyard, screaming and stamping their feet. "Strega! Strega!" they screeched and spit. My father had to separate them. In the afternoon we put my mother and my brothers and the still-outraged Iole on the train at Orbetello, and my father and I drove the car back to Rome.

We left Italy at the beginning of September. I had been enrolled by mail in the Masters School in Dobbs Ferry, south of Scarborough, and we had all worn out the travel euphoria that followed our first homesickness. We sailed on the *Constitution* from Genoa, and Iole came with us, leaving her reluctant fiancé behind. It was an unexceptional voyage; the captain was interested in getting to New York as fast as possible. The Schoaleses met us at the docks and we went through customs without incident, although Giuseppe and Pepe Le Moco kept poking their whiskers out of holes they had chewed in the paper bag around their cage. It didn't matter. My father had provided them with health certificates from the Italian government, complete with seals and signatures and red ribbons. We were about to become respectable.

Thirteen

I CAN SEE NOW that our year in Italy was a kind of turning point in my father's career and in our life as a family. The late fifties, after our return, marked the beginning of his professional success, his relative financial solvency, and his alcoholism. But in fact the transition wasn't so neat. The changes happened over a period of about five years, and climaxed when we left the house at Beechwood and established ourselves in our own house five miles north on a ridge above the Hudson.

It had taken my father twenty-five years to publish a novel and two collections of short stories. The success of *The Wapshot Chronicle* seemed to increase his energy as well as his confidence. In 1959, a year after *The Wapshot Chronicle* won the National Book Award, he finished the suburban stories in *The Housebreaker of Shady Hill*. Another collection, *Some People, Places, and Things That Will Not Appear in My Next Novel*, came out in 1961, and by 1963 he finished his next novel, *The Wapshot Scandal*. It was published in 1964, along with another collection of stories, *The Brigadier and the Golf Widow*. He also had two sojourns in Hollywood working for Jerry Wald and Twentieth Century–Fox on the adaptation of a D. H. Lawrence novel, *The Lost Girl*.

My mother's father died at the end of the summer in 1959, and this exacerbated the strains on my parents' marriage. There was a lot of talk about divorce. Tension with the editors at *The New Yorker* also increased. As my father became more prolific and more successful, his feeling that he was being underpaid and badly treated by the magazine grew. To deal with all this, he added a moderate consumption of Valium and Librium to his already considerable intake of alcohol. There was a lot of fighting in those years — at the dinner table, on the lawns, around the swimming pool. I was that most miserable of human beings, an adolescent, and after three unsuccessful years at the Masters School I transferred to the Woodstock Country School in South Woodstock, Vermont. I was glad to be away from home and very happy with the school. My father had wanted me to go to Masters, and he didn't hide his disappointment. Perhaps he hoped I would have the security and confidence that shines from the faces of the top girls in schools like that, or maybe he was just a snob. We fought bitterly.

"S. comes home with the news that she is on some sort of probation," he wrote in his journal when I was a junior at Masters, a few months after my grandfather died. "Her negativism, her digressive negativism, are thought to be bad attitudes in class. Our conversation begins in soft voices, but then I begin to shout. She cries and throws herself onto her bed, I order her to get up and eat her dinner and tell her that if this was in Italy I would hit her over the head with a piece of wood and Fred, catching the harsh or ugly notes in my voice begins to cry. We sit down to a gloomy table.

I read. At eight o'clock sharp the wind springs out of the north with gale force, an inundation of snow and rain. S. goes for a walk in the storm. Later I speak with her. 'I'm indifferent,' she says. 'I'm a mass of intelligence adrift. I don't care if I sleep in the street.' 'Oh, you don't,' say I as the wind flings the rain against the windows. 'Would you like to go out and sleep in the street this evening?' Here is sarcasm, fruitless and obscene."

We were all a little miserable, and the misery seemed to focus on the house in Scarborough. It no longer seemed all right to be living in a damp rented house on someone else's land. On the other hand, trying to find a house they wanted to buy, own, and live in permanently really put my parents up against their dreams and secret wishes. They weren't at all casual about sinking their savings and a lot of borrowed money into property. This loomed as an irrevocable act, a gesture of maturity and stability, an admission of age. To buy a house is one kind of statement of who you are and what you really want. It's a commitment, and a confession — not at all like "just renting," or "living here for a few years."

My father wanted the kind of grassy elegance and spacious architecture that he was accustomed to by now — but he wasn't sure he wanted to own it. He *was* sure that he couldn't afford it. My mother hated the idea of pretension, grandeur, or demonstrations of wealth or elegance. At the same time she had a weakness for luxury and beautiful things. Cramped spaces and squalor made her feel angry and put-upon. They were both trying to live up to some fantasy of lost abundance and grace and at the same time furiously denying that they were interested in such things — just in case it didn't work out, I suppose. At first my father settled on the grand but shabby place on Union Avenue in Saratoga. My mother vetoed that. Then she found a four-story Vic-

torian mansion on a hillside in Tarrytown. My father said
he couldn't afford it. The discovery of the house they finally
bought in 1960 did nothing to resolve the conflict. Originally built in 1799 by a Hudson River boatman named
Benjamin B. Acker, it is a lovely stone-ended house tucked
away in a private valley, with its own ponds and plantings
and orchard.

Sometimes my mother would say that she had seen this
house in her dreams, exactly as it was, even before they
found it. My father would then complain that it was too
grand and much too expensive, but if it made her happy
he was willing to go along with it, although of course it
meant he would have to work twice as hard. On other occasions, my father would say that once he had seen the house
he knew it was the only place he could live. My mother
would then complain that it was pretentious and too grand
and that she would have been just as happy in an ordinary
suburban development house.

Milton Greenstein, the lawyer who acts as counsel for
The New Yorker, may have clinched the deal when he made
a remark passed on to my father by Bill Maxwell in a
moment of indiscretion. Greenstein, Maxwell says, had
expressed the opinion that it was a mistake for free-lance
writers to own property. According to my father, he had
asked if *The New Yorker* would cosign a bank mortgage
for some of the $37,500 asking price and Greenstein had
answered: "What makes John think a writer can live in a
house like that?"

In the end, the down payment came from my mother's
savings and the money my father made in Hollywood, and
the Schoaleses cosigned the mortgage. The question of
whether or not to buy the house was settled, and we moved
in February of 1961, but the other problems remained.

"I come up against the picturesqueness of this house I

own," my father wrote in his journal. "My inability to possess it, to enjoy it, to take it for what it is. It is a warm day in the spring. I take off the storm windows so that the Dutch doors east and west stand open and the freshness of the afternoon flows through the rooms. The west doors frame the willows and the draw down toward the Hudson. The east doors frame the woods and the white water of the brook. Standing in the kitchen I can see the yellow walls of the dining room, the gleaming surface of the table, the blue dishes grandfather brought back from China, and I find these effects offensive. It is the vitality of the landscape I tell myself that I respond to, the vitality of the earth and not these picturesque arrangements; orchids in the library where a fire burns . . . somehow to admire this house seems like admiring my own face in a mirror. . . . So I come back to the fact that a writer does not possess a house: or that this house is a house and nothing but a house."

The house had a name — "Afterwhiles" — engraved on its twin stone gateposts. To show that he didn't care about that, and also to draw attention to it, my father always called it "Meanwhiles." To show that *she* didn't care, my mother suggested that it be renamed "The Grecian Earn."

Appearances. We were all told that appearances were not important, but no one believed it for a minute. My father described everyone and everything in terms of appearances. Women either "looked like something" or were "very attractive" or "great blondes," or they weren't. Men were "dressy" or "seedy" or "all boy," or they had a "good tan" or a "prison pallor" or in some cases a "large nose (breeding)" or "something wrong around the eyes." Restaurants, parties, and literary events were defined by "the crowd," which was "in evening clothes" or had "women with ornaments in their hair" or "good jewelry" or was "shabby." Even drinks were "brown" if they were strong and "pale" if they were watery.

My father was a spiritual man, a man who talked easily about good and evil, and the need for a transcendent vision in literature, and the importance of having some ultimate usefulness, and man's struggle to be illustrious. Religious terminology tripped easily off his tongue; and many of his experiences seemed to take on a kind of mythic dimension in his own mind. But it was always my observation that he took pretty women to be sweet-natured, and that he often concluded that plain women were unpleasant or abrasive. He adored Jacqueline Kennedy and hated Jeane Kirkpatrick. Of course he knew about bitchery, and he knew that everyone said that beauty is only skin deep and that handsome is as handsome does and that the Colonel's Lady and Kitty O'Grady are sisters under the skin. It was just hard for him to believe. He taught us, perhaps without meaning to, that appearances are crucially important — not because one is judged by them so much, but because they represent some inner dignity, some statement about a way of meeting the world. To "look like something," as he often put it, wasn't just a question of vanity; it was itself a kind of spiritual statement. To look like something was to be somebody. My father's belief in the importance of appearances often governed his actions.

Ten years after my parents moved to Ossining, my father telephoned me one evening to say that he was planning to leave my mother and marry someone else. Although he had often threatened to leave my mother, this was the first time he had specifically announced that he was engaged to another woman. (It wasn't the last time.) My husband and I were living in the country then. It was dark outside, but I could see the outlines of the trees swaying in the wind. Beyond them the light above the horizon glowered at the end of day.

"How come?" I said.

He explained that he had just returned from New York, where he had spent the afternoon with this other woman, and that she wanted to marry him. "She's one of the most beautiful women in the world," he said, "and she wants to marry me."

"So?" I said.

"When the most beautiful woman in the world wants to marry you, how can you say no?"

"You just do," I said.

Naturally, my father had expected his only daughter to be a beauty. He imagined me dazzling New York society and making a brilliant match. He imagined taking me to the racetrack at Saratoga and having everyone crane their necks and murmur to each other, asking who the stunning young girl with John might be. He imagined us leading the Boston June Cotillon. His journals include fantasies about conversations with the father of the groom — a Vanderbilt, a Biddle, a Cabot — in which the old gentleman explains the social and financial obligations I will have as his son's bride and my father assures him that I am up to it. When I was born, my mother says, it was my father who decided to name me Susan. "She'll have long blonde hair and drive a sports car and we'll call her Susie," he said.

They did call me Susie, but otherwise I defied my father's fantasies. As an adolescent I was dumpy, plagued by acne, slumped over, and alternately shy and aggressive, and my lank straight brown hair was always in my eyes. As my friendship with my father deepened from our talks and going on trips or to parties together — my mother was often too busy to go — the conflict over my looks intensified. My father seemed to think that if I lost weight, curled my hair, and stood up straight, my academic problems would evaporate and I would be surrounded by the handsome and adoring suitors who seemed so elusive. The fact that he may have been right made the situation even worse.

The few times my male classmates did ask me for dates, they were met at the door by my father — transparently eager, instead of the stern, law-abiding parent they expected. He was positively euphoric with gratitude and relief. He thanked them profusely for asking me out and urged them to keep me out as late as they liked. It was unsettling. They always brought me home early, and they never came back.

When I finally managed to lure a few men home from college for weekends, though, my father didn't appear to be at all pleased. He was cool and courtly as long as there was no overt display of affection. Hand holding, kissing, and even open flirtatiousness made him furious. He liked to invite my boyfriends off with him to go scything in the meadow or work on a felled tree with the chain saw or clear some brush out behind the pine trees. I don't know what happened out there, but they always came back in a rage. When I fell in love at last and brought my true love home from school to visit, there were terrible scenes — almost as terrible as the angry scenes from the days when I didn't have a date.

I see now that my father was expressing his own confusion about sex. What seemed innocent necking to me looked not at all innocent to him. He knew better. My father was a man with intense and polymorphous appetites that caused him tremendous guilt and self-loathing. His desires could poison his image of the pure life he wanted, or they could create it. For him, sexual excitement was charged with the possibility of supreme pleasure and revolting lewdness. Here were the forces of good and the forces of evil combined and equal in one powerful human desire. No wonder there were scenes.

Fourteen

T HERE IS THE PRESENCE of a father — stern, unintelligent and with a gamey odor — but a force of counsel and support that would have carried one, well-equipped, into manhood," my father wrote in his journal. "One does not invest the image with brilliance or wealth; it is simply a man in a salt and pepper tweed, sometimes loving, sometimes irascible and sometimes drunk but always responsible to his son."

My father didn't have this ideal, tweedy parent he dreamed of in his journal who would have "equipped him for manhood." He spent much of his life looking for counsel and support from surrogate fathers and ultimately, painfully, rejecting them. His brother Fred was the first character in this drama, as my father relived the pattern of his own abandonment, salvation, and flight again and again and again. Malcolm Cowley was one of these parental figures, as was Elizabeth Ames at Yaddo. Perhaps the most important older men in his life, sources of extensive "support and counsel," were my mother's father — Winter, as my father called him — and the editors at *The New Yorker*, particularly

Bill Maxwell. One had custody of his wife, as it were, and the others had custody of his work. In the years between 1957 and 1963 my father turned his back on both of these forces of support.

✳   ✳   ✳

By the time my grandfather died in 1959, his friendship with my father was over. My mother always said that when Winter asked for my father on his deathbed, my father refused to go. Sometimes she added that she could never forgive him for this. It was the angry last act of what had been a passionate alliance between my father and his father-in-law. Treetops had been a paradise for my father, and Winter and Polly had treated him like a son — certainly better than they treated their own sons.

In the 1940s and 1950s Treetops was run like an old-fashioned estate. There were always houseguests, and the staff included a cook with an assistant, two gardeners, a handyman, a nurse or a nanny or a "mamselle," or all three, depending on which children were in residence, and my grandmother's personal lady's maid, Marie de Grasse. In the morning my grandmother would dress in gardening clothes — a broadbrim hat, a pale blue shirt, and "old" lightweight silk trousers — and select flowers from her four flower gardens for the central arrangement at the Stone House, the main house on the property, where she lived with my grandfather.

She was an old-time lady: a crack tennis player, a good swimmer (she always wore a hat and bathing shoes), a great martini drinker, a mother of four, a woman who knew above all things how to enjoy herself — and a woman who had really never been asked to do anything else. She always "looked like something." I don't think it ever occurred to her that there was another way to live, or that there were goals for a woman outside of friends and family and having, my dear, an absolutely wonderful time. I think she was one of the most contented women I have ever known, contented in a way that isn't possible anymore. Her achievements matched her expectations as though they had been tailored for each other by Worth.

Polly and my father shared a passion for gossip, backgammon, witty satires of people they knew, and straight gin. What fun they had together down at the Stone House, telling stories on the absent members of the family as they set up the board, shook the first dice out of the heavy leather backgammon cups, and poured their first martinis from the shaker into their iceless triangular glasses. The mantelpiece at Treetops still holds a big copper martini pitcher inscribed "The Pauline Whitney Winternitz Backgammon Award." What fun they had, nipping into town in the Buick (my grandfather's car) or the Studebaker (my grandmother's) for special treats not to be shared with their siblings and cousins and children who sulked in the smaller cottages up the hill. My father liked to tell stories about my grandfather stuffing himself with his favorite Polish sausage at martini time and then, at dinner distastefully pushing away the specially prepared dishes set in front of him while his children anxiously urged him to eat something.

"For him I also feel a deep affection," my father wrote of Winter in the early fifties. "I think he feels something like this for me. We are alike, I think — at least while we are together we seem alike. We are both eccentric. In his case there is something heartening to me in seeing an impulsive and eccentric nature enjoying his considerable success. He is given to storms of petulance and so am I. His deviousness fascinates me. And with both of us, our relationship, at moments, seems dominated by a passion of penitence. In his kindness for me there is penitence for all the unkindnesses he had done to his sons. In my patience with him there is penitence for the unkindness I showed my father."

My father was sarcastic; my grandfather easily outdid him. Often important guests would be invited up to Tree-tops from Yale or from Washington, D.C., where my grand-father went to work at the National Research Council after he left New Haven. Not infrequently, the guests left early. They couldn't take the cutting and constant fire of critical commentary my grandfather kept up. He was funny, but he was also cruel. My father admired this. He liked to say that my grandfather's award citations at Yale had often left the honorees in tears. According to him, the mention of my grandfather's name in certain circles caused people to lay down their lives for you — or to burst into humiliated sobs. This image, the image of a successful and brilliant man who was so powerful, such a force, that he was either loved or hated, was very evocative for all of us. At first my father created a model from this image, and he adored it. Later he changed his mind.

My grandfather was certainly a violent and volatile man. I saw him time and time again gripped by uncontrollable rages: at a slow traffic cop, at an umbrella salesman who had failed to repair his umbrella, at a gas-station attendant who forgot to check the oil. He taught his children to swim by throwing them off the raft at Treetops (one of them never wanted to go in the water again), and he beat his sons with a belt until they bled. But he could also be profoundly gen-erous and supportive. I remember him gently binding or swabbing my childhood scrapes and cuts and hornet stings, and giving me just the books I longed for, and staying up at night with me to talk about our family and especially my real grandmother, his wife who had died. He taught me to recite the Lord's Prayer and Lewis Carroll's "Jabberwocky" by heart, and the year before he died, he gave me my grandmother's gold and onyx girlhood ring.

As Winter got older, my father seemed to see more and more of his deviousness and less of his generosity. At first it began to seem to him that he and my mother were expected to act the parts of dutiful children when they were at Treetops. This became harder and harder for him. He began to see the family, with its backbiting and gossiping and drinking, as a negative force on his work — and he began to feel that my grandfather's presence had a destructive effect on his own marriage and children. By the early 1950s, he had started returning to Scarborough alone for two or three weeks every summer to write.

As his connection to my mother became more complicated and difficult, my father became convinced that her moods were the irrational result of injuries she had sustained in childhood. My grandfather, who had inflicted these injuries, became the villain. Instead of paradise, Treetops began to look like a kind of hell peopled by self-righteous cripples who lived in the past. My father spent less and less time there. "I have come to think of Winter as the king of a Hades where M. must spend perhaps half her time," he wrote, neatly comparing my mother to Persephone as my grandfather lay dying. "There is no question that he is a source of darkness in our affairs."

In 1959, the summer my grandfather was dying, my father had gone to visit old friends in Italy. He had a harrowing flight back to New York — the plane's engines caught fire over the Atlantic. At one point the door to the cockpit flew open and he noticed that the pilot was wearing a life jacket. They were forced to return to Orly Airport in Paris and change planes. He had escaped death, but no one met him

at the airport. He took the train out to Scarborough and
walked up the hill to the house. We were all in New Hampshire, except for Iole and the baby. There was no one to ask
about my father's trip, no one to be glad that he was still
among the living, no one to hear his hair-raising stories
about the flight. When he called my mother at Treetops, she
was too upset about her father to pay much attention.

I often asked my father why he didn't go to my grandfather when he was dying. Sometimes he would say that he
didn't realize how sick Winter was — the old man was an
inspired faker — and that he was sorry. Other times he
admitted that he felt Winter had become a negative force
on our family. A few times he said that he had turned against
my grandfather because of his cruelty to me. He was right,
of course, about my mother's childhood experiences having
an effect on her marriage, and he was also right in feeling
excluded from her problems with her father. That such
circumstances are almost universal didn't make any difference to him. He was jealous and probably angry. In the end,
he just didn't want to go, and that was that.

❋　　❋　　❋

My father had a naive faith in ordinary people's benevolence
and good nature, and this seemed to attract benevolence and
good nature. Strangers bought him drinks and offered him
rides. Casual acquaintances lent him money; circumstances
seemed to favor him with fortune, and he was thrilled and
exhilarated by these chance acts of kindness and generosity.
But with the people closest to him, his expectations were
very different. He had a hair-trigger sense of injustice, and
his life story as he told it sometimes seemed to consist of a
series of grave injustices by friends, family, or close asso-
ciates, magically overcome by the kindness of strangers and
by his own talent and charm.

Under the circumstances, it was almost inevitable that there would come a time when my father broke away from his editors at *The New Yorker* and from everything the magazine had represented for him. *The New Yorker* has always been an eccentric institution. It is also one of American journalism's quirkiest success stories. Since it was started in 1925 by Harold Ross, a journalist from Aspen, Colorado, and Raoul Fleischmann, of the Fleischmann yeast family, it has had only two editors: Ross, a brilliant, skeptical, and abrasive character whose eccentricities and discernment have made him a legend, and William Shawn, whose reticence and shyness almost seem to make him Ross's opposite, and who has in his very different way also commanded the respect of the magazine's editors and writers. Ross was profane, and sometimes, when exasperated, yelled at people. Shawn's voice is a whisper. Ross treated his writers as if they were beloved and wayward children. Shawn treats them with exaggerated and courtly respect. But both men oversaw every aspect of the magazine, read every story, and approved every cartoon, and together they built it from a flaky humor magazine into a literary weekly that has a style and seriousness unique in this country.

People visiting the *New Yorker* offices on the eighteenth floor (the writers' floor) of the building on Forty-third Street are often disappointed. The elevator opens onto a hallway that looks like a combination yard sale and furniture warehouse. Old couches and desks and empty water-cooler jugs are stacked in the corners. A receptionist sits in a glass cubicle and buzzes the elect through a grimy door into the inner sanctum. The shabby offices, and the worn sofas grouped in an alcove and looking as if they were an afterthought, do not reflect the excellence of the staff and its contributors, nor the financial success of the product. At *The New Yorker* such things are not important.

Every writer has some relationship with an editor or two, but at *The New Yorker* these bonds are often unusually close. This was certainly true in my father's case. His feelings about his editors there — Gus Lobrano and Bill Maxwell — were much more than professional. If my father was looking for a father, *The New Yorker* was willing. Both Lobrano and Maxwell became close friends of his. He went fishing in Canada with Gus, and Bill and Emily Maxwell saw my parents often. Bill was four years older than my father, and a novelist as well as an editor — he and my father had been friends since they started out as writers together in New York City in the 1930s. Sometimes Maxwell's editing consisted of punctuation and spelling corrections or changes for clarity, but other times he or Lobrano suggested more extensive revisions. My father had tremendous respect for Maxwell as a writer and as a friend, and he took these editing suggestions very much to heart. When *The New Yorker* rejected his stories, he often just threw them out.

The *New Yorker* system of payment compounds the atmosphere of benevolent paternalism the magazine's editors sometimes foster. Few people understand it. Few writers know what other writers are paid, and many aren't even sure what they will be paid. Payment for what the magazine calls "long fact" (nonfiction) has often been lower at other magazines, while payment for fiction has often been higher. Fiction writers do not have offices at *The New Yorker*; fact writers do have offices. My father said that this was because Ross had felt that improvisation and struggle were good for fiction writers — my father could have done with a little less of both.

When fiction writers become steady contributors to the magazine, they are offered a "first look" or "first reading" agreement — a contract for which they receive token pay-

ment and the magazine gets right of first refusal on anything they write. The contract is renewed annually, and it
also specifies the writer's minimum word rate for that year.
In 1979, for instance, my father's word rate was forty-seven
cents a word. A complicated bonus system rewards the
writer for the quantity of stories published in the magazine
each year, and this can amount to a twenty-five percent
increase in the writer's annual income. Because Ross wanted
to encourage short pieces of fiction, writers were paid at one
rate up to 1500 words and at a lower rate for the remainder
of the piece. There were also different pay rates based on
the editor's grading of a story from A down to C minus.
(This evaluation was not passed on to the writers.) During
the years my father wrote for the magazine, COLA, or Cost
Of Living Allowance, was also added to the writer's story
fee. Some writers also had drawing accounts, or other special
arrangements that enabled them to borrow against future
work.

Undoubtedly this Byzantine system was established for
the benefit of writers, but in my father's case, at least, its
ultimate result was confusion and resentment. The checks
he received for stories were sometimes larger than he had
anticipated, but they were often smaller, and the frustration
of the latter situation hardly made up for the pleasure of
the former. In 1959, for instance, he published six stories in
the magazine and received checks as diverse as $792 for
"A Woman Without a Country" and $2170 for "The Events
of That Easter." This situation led to misunderstanding,
especially since discussions of money seemed to be both
ungentlemanly and *infra dig* at the magazine. Sometimes
my father expected a large check for a long story, only to
find that it had been applied to money taken from his drawing account. Other times money that he assumed was pay-

ment, or a bonus, or a COLA check, turned out to be an advance. *The New Yorker* probably didn't expect anyone to make a living out of writing fiction in those days, and most fiction contributors turned in two or three stories a year. But my father had devoted most of his considerable creative energy to writing short stories for the magazine, and he expected more than they were willing to give. The money they paid him just wasn't enough to live on — even in the years when we children were in public schools and the family in a rented house. In some years my father published ten stories in the magazine, but his annual income was often less than $10,000. He maintained a first-look contract with the magazine (he had one of the first such contracts) from 1935 until his death in 1982 — almost fifty years. His total income from *The New Yorker* during that time was $126,547.09 plus $46,167.90 from the COLA. In the early 1960s, as his financial needs became more pressing and his reputation grew, *The New Yorker* rates began to seem less adequate and their payment system even more infuriating. It was clear that he could get more money elsewhere.

More seriously, a real disagreement was developing over what my father wanted to do with the short story form, and what the *New Yorker* editors felt was appropriate and believable. My father started to experiment, to stretch the traditional story form and to bring some mythic dimension to everyday events — to explore experience as metaphor and vice versa.

"His stories collided with the *New Yorker* idea of fiction," Bill Maxwell told me. "Character as a confining force got less and less strong in his work. He extricated himself from ordinary realism. There was nothing in the contemporary scene that he didn't sweep up and use in his stories, and sometimes I just stood there with my mouth open."

My father's use of character and metaphor now seem relatively conservative, but fiction at *The New Yorker* in the 1950s and early 1960s had not changed much from fiction as it always — or usually — had been. "He tried things that we felt just weren't possible," Maxwell says. "It turned out that anything was possible."

The situation came to a head a few days before Christmas in 1963. It was the day, in fact, that my father finished writing "The Swimmer," a story in which traditional realism is thoroughly transcended. Delivering the manuscript to Maxwell at the *New Yorker* office, my father decided he would make his plea for more money. He was paying two private-school tuitions (I was at Brown University, Ben at the Scarborough School, and Fred in the local public school) and the monthly mortgage and was also coping with repairs on a very old house and the rising cost of almost everything.

He loved to tell the story of what happened that afternoon, and he made it very funny — as if telling it over and over again would somehow make it all right. When he told it, he often set it on Christmas Eve and threw in a snowstorm and the suggestion that he couldn't afford to buy presents for his children. When he got to Maxwell's office, he patiently explained the situation. He wanted to continue writing for the magazine. He had been publishing in the magazine for almost thirty years. He loved working with Bill. But he desperately needed more money — he had to have more money. Maxwell said no. As a part-time editor, he did not have the power to change the payment system. When my father persisted, Maxwell suggested that he might see if he could do better elsewhere.

Distraught, my father left the office and walked down Forty-fourth Street through the falling snow to a pay phone. He had no official literary agent — he hadn't thought he

needed one, really — but he called Candida Donadio, who
was just making a name for herself at the Russell & Volken-
ing agency. He fed a dime into the phone and got through
to Candida and explained the situation.

"Stay right there," she said. A few minutes later, the pay
phone rang. It was Candida, saying that *The Saturday
Evening Post* would pay $24,000 for a first-look contract and
four stories a year. This was almost three times his average
New Yorker income, and ten times what their first-look contract guaranteed. *The Saturday Evening Post* was ready to
negotiate upward, Candida said.

It was with some trepidation that my father made his way
back through the crowds of Christmas shoppers and merry-
makers to Bill Maxwell's office. When he told Maxwell what
had happened, there was great consternation, he said. There
were telephone calls and hurried conferences. The magazine
offered to increase the payment for his first-look contract —
to another minimal figure — and it was suggested that the
editors wouldn't be draconian about it if my father occasionally published elsewhere. Mr. Shawn and the magazine's
treasurer, Hawley Truax, both came down to reason with
him. Truax, my father said, anxiously offered him bonuses:
the key to the men's room and all the bread and cheese he
could eat. He said he would think it over, and he took the
train back out to Ossining.

It tells you a lot about my father that he stayed at *The
New Yorker*. He signed the *New Yorker* contract every year
for the rest of his life, but he wrote fewer stories and those
he wrote were often rejected. In the eighteen years after
The New Yorker published "The Swimmer," only seven
Cheever stories appeared in the magazine (almost a hundred
had appeared in the eighteen years before that). Certainly
one of the reasons my father stayed was his affection for

Bill Maxwell. Sometimes, in inveighing against *The New Yorker*, he would leave Maxwell out of it, as if it was something Maxwell had no part in. They continued to write to each other and see each other occasionally, but the intensity of their friendship was never renewed.

My father made the story of his break with the magazine a triumphant comedy, and he told it again and again. I think he was trying to convince himself that he had behaved in the only way he could have. Who knows what really happened that day? Bill Maxwell says there was a quarrel about money and that, to his distress, the magazine's payment system simply did not allow him to pay my father more. As a friend, he believed that my father needed money, and so, as a friend, he suggested that someone else might be able to pay him more. He knew about the *Saturday Evening Post* offer, but there was nothing he could do.

"Then I ask Bill for more money, a scene that is embarrassing for both of us," my father wrote in his journal. "Like many men of fifty I am obliged to ask for a raise and like many men of fifty I am confronted with a blameless, monolithic and capricious organization, hobbled it seems by its own prosperity. The organizations of men, like men themselves, seem subject to deafness, near-sightedness, lameness and involuntary cruelty. We seem tragically unable to help one another; to understand one another. I am accused of improvidence and make several long speeches about how I am harassed by indebtedness. *The Post* has offered me twenty-four thousand; *The New Yorker* has offered me twenty-five hundred and I will take the latter. I'm not sure why."

Fifteen

MY FATHER DIDN'T LIKE confrontations. Superior authority made him alternately resentful and timid. He expressed his anger with quiet, scathing sarcasm. In verbal disagreements, his mind often quickly imagined and assimilated the other point of view, making his own seem relatively weak and one-sided. It wasn't that he gave in; he just withdrew from the field. He rarely raised his voice, and I can only remember him throwing something once: "Can't you even tell the silver from the stainless steel, for Christ's sake?" he hissed, heaving the pieces I had dried and misplaced across the little kitchen of the house in Scarborough. The story of how I escaped from him the last time he tried to spank me is a family legend. I remember it vividly: my terrified skid around the wing chair in the living room, my vault over the sofa next to the dining room table, and my final leap into my bedroom, where I slammed and locked the door. By the time I came out, we were all able to agree that I was too old to be spanked. No one remembers what I had done in the first place.

My father usually kept his distance. After I became an adult, he carefully avoided arguments, staying away from subjects he knew we disagreed on such as contemporary art, the value of psychoanalysis, and the novels of John Fowles. He was staunchly apolitical. Aside from voting the Democratic ticket every four years and having predictable liberal reactions to candidates and policies, he assiduously avoided the issues. In the late 1960s when many of his friends and colleagues opposed the war in Vietnam, my father privately agreed with them. Publicly, he abstained.

"A march on Washington to protest the war in Vietnam," he wrote after a group of fellow writers marched across the Mall and up to the Lincoln Memorial in 1966. "I talk much against the war, but I will not march because I am lazy, suffer from agoraphobia, will probably have a hangover, am afraid of the reactionary bullies who will hiss and boo me, afraid of any public commitment of my opinions, am shy, timid, a born bystander etc. . . . Actually, I seem unable to think of this demonstration as useful beyond the personal usefulness of making a physical declaration of where one stands."

In the 1960s and 1970s my father visited Russia three times, always at the invitation of the Soviet government or the government-controlled writers' union. Although he saw the situation of the Russian dissidents at first hand, he tried his hardest to keep his observations and opinions private and to avoid being used for propaganda purposes either by the government or by those against it. Even in that situation, he remained apolitical and consistently refused to speak for or against anyone or anything. His name never appeared on the petitions circulated by American writers in support of the Russian dissidents. One of his closest friends in Russia was Tanya Litvinov, the daughter of former commissar of foreign affairs Maxim Litvinov, and the woman who had translated most of my father's work into Russian. His work sold well in Russia — he refused to discuss the possibility that this was because its view of the capitalist United States could be very negative — and he had a lot of money in roubles that he was unable to take out of the country. Once, at dinner with Tanya in Moscow, he offered her this extra money. She could buy something for herself or her husband, he suggested; she could get her teeth fixed or find a warm winter coat. Tanya told him that if she took the money she would donate it to help publish *Samizdats* — dissident underground books and papers. My father withdrew his offer.

The angriest I can remember him being in recent years was during a conversation we had about Saul Bellow's novel *Humboldt's Gift*, which was published in 1975. After I had read and admired the book, I was fascinated to hear through the literary grapevine that it was based on Bellow's experience at Princeton, and that the main character was drawn from the poet Delmore Schwartz. I couldn't wait to tell my father, but instead of being interested, he was furious.

"That's the kind of speculation I abhor," he said. When he was angry, his voice got cold and sharp and he used old-fashioned language. "The book is a great work of fiction, it cannot be reduced to gossip." I always learned something from my father's anger. I can still tell sterling from stainless at a hundred feet.

Our family had a cat named Delmore Schwartz, and my father hated him. His descriptions of our household animals and their feelings, as well as his use of voices he attributed to them, were sometimes unusually revealing. His friends and family got letters from the Cheever dogs, complete with hilarious misspellings, describing the family goings-on from their point of view. Other letters almost always mentioned the dogs, whom he loved, or the cats, whom he didn't.

Delmore himself was the unwanted gift of my father's old friend Josie Herbst, who brought him with her when she came for lunch one day in 1960. Josie said the cat was a kitten named Blackie who had been owned by her friend Elizabeth Pollet, the former wife of Delmore Schwartz. My father suspected Josie of lying about the cat's age; he suspected her of unloading an aged, bad-tempered animal on her country friends. The evidence supported him. Blackie the kitten was a large animal with a worn coat and only half a tail. My father made up a past for the cat. Schwartz had locked him in a bathroom for months at a time; he had lost his tail in an accident with a refrigerator door. Blackie was renamed Delmore.

Josie had never made any money, and this kept the edge on her pro-labor 1930s politics. It was the responsibility of the rich to care for the poor, she felt. My father was rich, Delmore was poor. My father accepted this responsibility, but with reluctance. At first, Delmore was used as comic relief. At school in Woodstock, and later at college in Providence, Rhode Island, I got letters from my father about how he had washed the storm windows so well that Delmore had tried to jump through one and folded up like an accordion, or how Delmore had tried to leap from the bathtub to the windowsill and landed in the toilet. Other people's cats caught mice. Delmore sulkily coexisted with the mice and shrews that proliferated in the pantry and the kitchen cupboards. When he did catch a mouse, he was sure to leave it in the bathtub or in one of my father's shoes. Gradually Delmore became a scapegoat as well as a clown. It was Delmore who woke my parents with his angry shrieks at dawn, and who continued to yowl when my father went downstairs, presented him with a breakfast he refused to eat, and finally drop-kicked him out the kitchen door. It was Delmore who left mutilated bird carcasses on the front stairs when the Canfields came over for dinner from Bedford or when the Steegmullers arrived for lunch in their Rolls-Royce. It was Delmore who made a point of relieving himself in the darkest parts of the hallway so that you couldn't see it until you — or a guest — had stepped in it. He even turned up as the sinister black cat in *Bullet Park*. When Hammer's cat comes home smelling of perfume, Hammer follows the scent and the cat into trouble. In 1964, when my father telephoned me at college to say that Delmore was dead, his first words were, "I want you to know that I didn't have anything to do with it."

My father loved dogs. Cassiopeia, the black Labrador puppy he bought from a litter out of Phil Boyer's bitch Sable of Teatown in 1952, became his muse, his companion, his faithful and discreet confidante. Cassie was not really a dog at all but a dowager countess with all the airs of a stingy aristocrat, my father would explain to anyone who cared to listen. She and our next dog, Flora Macdonald (named for the woman who helped Bonnie Prince Charlie escape from Scotland), were actually "formerly dorgs" — a term he had invented to explain the fact that they were really people temporarily trapped in hairy, rotund bodies. He had a special relationship with many medium-sized or large dogs (small dogs were too much like cats). He loved Arthur Spear's Minerva (Flora's daughter), and the Maxwells' Daisy, and the Swopes' Mowena, and Gene and Clare Thaw's Kelly, and my two golden retrievers Maisie and Bathsheba (everyone else called Bathsheba "Sheba," but my father felt that she liked to be called by her full name), and the Boyers' Ezekiel, whom we had as a puppy because he was the son of our Labrador Cassiopeia.

"Dear Zeke," my father wrote to him at the Boyers', in what he imagined was Cassie's inimitable tone.

it was very good to hear from you. you will nevr know how much yr lettrs mean to me now that i am nearing the end of my journey. oh i know you will say mother dere, no, no, no, but the truth is that yr mother has got so weak in these last months that she can no longer raise herself up to the lid of an average-sized garbage pail. . . . daisy maxwell [the Maxwells' yellow Labrador] came to visit. she is yellow all over and committed several discourtesies that I do not choose to describe. The old fool got smeared and invited his publisher [Cass Canfield] to dinner. This publisher is a rich old man named Cassie and so naturally there were a lot of mix ups such as when the old fool would shout cassie get your face out of the cracker dish or cassie shut up. mrs. swope was there and she giggled. they had pasta to eat with some kind of sauce that did not agree with me. pfffffrt, pffffrt all night long. i simply didn't shut my eyes once.

please try to enjoy yourself and try not to let the thought of your lonely impoverished and enfeebled old mother come between yourself and your happiness. look away from the body into truth and light.

yr loving Mother

He also described his own affection for Cassie in his journal.

The old dog, my love. The difficulties with upholstered furniture. How she began in her middle age to dislike long walks. Starting up the beach she seemed to enjoy herself but if you took an eye off her she would swing around and gallop back to the house. . . . That she always got to her feet when I entered the room. That she enjoyed men very much and was conspicuously indifferent to women. That her dislikes were marked and she definitely preferred people from traditional and if possible wealthy origins. That she had begun to resemble those imperious and somehow mannish women who devilled my youth; the dancing teacher, the banker's wife, the headmistress of the progressive school I attended. How when I was alone and heard her wandering through the house my feelings for her were of love and gratitude; that her heavy step put me to sleep. That she barked when I talked loudly to myself.

Cassie was put down by the vet in 1968, because she had become too crippled to walk, but when Flora died at home in my mother's arms, almost ten years later, there was a problem. My father wrapped her in burlap and put her on the porch bench, where the other dogs sniffed her apprehensively. The next day, my mother insisted that my father dig a grave for her. He had to drive to Vermont that evening to read at Bennington, and he explained that he didn't have the energy to do both. In the end, the man who came to mow the lawn dug the grave. Flora rests at the end of the rose garden, next to a chrysanthemum planted in her memory.

My father's last dog was a scruffy golden retriever of indeterminate age. For a long time I thought this dog would be the exception to my father's passion for the canine species, but I underestimated his perversity and the dog's well-masked charm. She was a boisterous, leggy, badly bred dog with a square head and a habit of dropping wet rocks on your feet. My parents inherited her when my brother Ben didn't want her anymore. She was named Tara, after Scarlett O'Hara's ancestral home in *Gone With the Wind*. My father decided that Tara was an unsuitable name for a dog, and he rechristened her "Edgar." Although this resulted in some sexual confusion, he usually referred to her as "him," altering the pronoun to go with her new name. The change seemed to give her oblivious stubbornness an endearing quality, and slowly Edgar became my father's dog just as Cassie and Flora had been before her. My father fed her and she slept at the foot of his bed. Edgar was photographed with my father for *Time* and *People* (her frequently successful efforts to knock over photographers notwithstanding); she appeared on book-jacket covers and in the newspapers.

"We are very close," my father wrote me about Edgar when I was living in France in 1978.

> He seems to feel it is his destiny to walk with me in these twilight years. When he wakes me, late at night, rooting noisily amongst his dingle-berries, we exchange the most profound and tender smiles before we both return to sleep. . . . In the evenings we watch the baseball games on TV and we both cry at triples. What has come between us is Tennis Balls.
>
> Edgar led me to believe that he enjoys Tennis Balls. We have a new neighbor named Townsend who will give me a can of tennis balls if I will lunch with him. Townsend likes to talk about how undeserved is his failure as a novelist. I get three balls. I give these to Edgar, one by one, and he hides them all over the place and brings for me to throw for him sharp rocks, black walnuts and an occasional tomato. When I lecture him on the fact that I have ruined my day for a tin of tennis balls he brings me more rocks and walnuts. I sometimes raise my voice and the neighbors and their friends all come out to listen. . . . I don't know where this will end.

Edgar was a sort of noble savage, I suppose, a canine version of the dumb innocent who is wiser than all the scholars and professors and learned doctors. In the end, her prescience was spooky. When my father came back from his first visit to Memorial Hospital in 1981, just after his disease had been diagnosed as cancer, Edgar abandoned her place at the foot of his bed and went to sleep in the living room. My father was terribly upset by this defection. Although none of us said it, it was as if Edgar knew that my father was going to die. It took us a few days to lure her back, but about a month after that Edgar started to cough. She wouldn't eat. One afternoon she got caught in the snow under my father's car, and although he could hardly walk, he crawled underneath to free her. Later my mother took her to the vet. The next day they did a series of X-rays, and the vet called to explain that Edgar had lung cancer. It was too late to do anything about it. She died in March of 1982.

Sixteen

W HEN I WAS ABOUT TWELVE I announced that I wanted
to be a writer and [my parents] said they would have to
think it over," my father told me when I interviewed him
for the *Newsweek* cover story in 1977. "After a couple of
days they said that I could be a writer as long as I didn't
seek wealth or fame. So I said that was not what I was
seeking — a remark I've often regretted."

Although the idea that the goal of an artist is incom-
patible with worldly success had been held by generations of
New England Yankees and their English forebears, it caused
quite a stir at *Newsweek* in the late 1970s. Why on earth
would my father's parents tell him not to seek wealth or
fame? Boston manners, Yankee purity and perversity, the
teachings of the Episcopal Church, and the Gospel According to Matthew where it says "Lay not up for yourselves
treasures here upon earth, where moth and rust doth cor-
rupt, and where thieves break through and steal!" seemed
almost archaic by 1977 in New York City. However desperate and impoverished my grandparents might have been,
they probably felt that wealth and fame were beneath them.

But there is so much emphasis on wealth and fame these days that the idea of going beyond these things has become profoundly romantic and noble — and very confusing. My father was as confused as anyone.

His aristocratic New England background was partly sham, and his patrician airs were mostly his own invention. He never came from the kind of fox-hunting gentleman's world that he encouraged people to construct for him. But my father's parents, for all their embittered shabbiness, were part of another generation — another century, really. They both had a kind of lunatic Yankee pride and rectitude that seems as outdated as memories of sailing ships and the China trade, steam locomotives and the acrid smell of smoke from factory chimneys along the Merrimack. In a lot of ways my father was still joined to that bygone world. He had a personal pride and a modesty and decency in dealing with other people that survived the twentieth century intact, like the Canton teapots on the corner shelves and the old ivory fan in the upstairs hallway that Captain Benjamin Hale Cheever had brought back from China.

"I think my mother would have been indignant," he wrote Bill Maxwell in 1965, when he won the American Academy of Arts and Letters' William Dean Howells Medal for *The Wapshot Scandal*. "I mean I think she would have claimed to be indignant as she would have claimed to have known Howells; and this may account for my own clumsiness but I do feel keenly that it is unsuitable. It is like giving a high jump prize to someone who can merely run. There are some people who positively thirst for medals but I seem not to have learned. . . . I am not a Wapshot of course but I was raised to believe that the acceptance of any honor was improper. As a child I used to wake in the night crying: No thank you, Oh no thank you."

In creating a gentleman's heritage for himself, my father

was justifying his own convictions. He wanted to be beyond money, but money buys paper and typewriters and lawns and people to mow them, and it pays school tuition and doctors' fees. He used to joke that he had taught us that small bills come out of the cold-water tap and large bills out of the hot-water tap. In other words, we didn't know the value of a dollar or a hundred dollars, and he was proud of that. For him, money was almost completely subjective; the value of the dollar fluctuated wildly depending on his state of mind. He was rich sometimes and he was poor sometimes, and both of these conditions were as dependent on his mood as they were on his net worth (which also fluctuated pretty wildly). Until the 1960s he was never rich by anyone's standards, but he sometimes felt rich and spent his money accordingly. I was sent to private school, but he never had any life insurance and we couldn't afford a car. We had a maid, and a private nurse when Ben was born. I took riding lessons and ballet lessons, but my father didn't have an office.

When he felt poor, the reverse happened. In 1953 I was taken out of private school and enrolled in public school, just as he had been. When he felt rich in 1965, my brother Fred was taken out of public school and enrolled in private school — with equally unhappy results. There were two or three years in the mid-1960s when my father made a good deal of money, but he never even thought about investment. The Federal Deposit Insurance Corporation covered up to $10,000 in the bank in those days, and my father deposited $10,000 in almost every bank in Westchester. He didn't keep records, of course, so he kept forgetting banks and feeling poor and then finding the savings books in odd places and feeling rich again. I'm not sure he knew the difference between principal and interest at that point. In the last few

years of his life, when he did invest some money, he couldn't
get over the fact that he was making money by doing nothing. It delighted him, because he felt he was getting away
with something.

In the last years of the 1950s and during the 1960s, my
father went from being a talented, struggling writer to being
an acknowledged, established success. By 1965, when *The
Wapshot Scandal* won the Howells Medal, he had won the
National Book Award and two Guggenheim Fellowships and
had been elected to the National Institute of Arts and Letters
and the prestigious Century Association, a men's club originally founded by artists, that occupies all four stories of a
Stanford White building on Forty-third Street. He had made
a million dollars, he had spent the weekend with Hugh
Hefner at the Playboy Mansion in Chicago, and he had been
received at the White House by President Lyndon Johnson
(he noticed that the president seemed very tired). In 1964 he
spent six weeks in Russia with John and Mary Updike on a
cultural-exchange mission. Frank and Eleanor Perry bought
the movie rights to "The Swimmer," and Burt Lancaster
agreed to star in it. Alan Pakula took an option on the
Wapshot novels. Pakula and his wife, the actress Hope
Lange, came for lunch, and Hope looked so pretty that my
father couldn't take his eyes off her. In 1964 a flattering oil
portrait of him appeared on the cover of *Time* magazine;
the equally flattering cover story, "Ovid in Ossining," was
written by his old friend Alwyn Lee and "researched" during a hilarious all-expenses-paid week of skiing at Stowe.
My father paid off some of the mortgage on the house and
bought himself a new car — a bright-red Karmann-Ghia
convertible. His marriage was still exciting, his children
were thriving, and we all made a lot of "Will success spoil
John Cheever?" jokes. Later, success and celebrity took a

big toll on my father and he became quite pompous about himself. But during these first moments of gratification it was impossible not to share his delight — and he wanted everyone to share it, too, giving money away and urging us to spend it. We had always teased my father about his reviews, and his "pervasive sweetness of heart" and "childlike sense of wonder," two reviewers' phrases, were often worked into the family jokes. Later, he stopped laughing at this kind of thing, but in the early 1960s he was still flexible and funny and as worried as anyone about the possible effects of success.

"After they put Daddy's picture on the cover of *Time*, he seemed to lose something," he wrote in his journal, imagining my thoughts. "I don't mean like Dorian Gray or anything but like a savage who thinks that if he is photographed he will have lost part of his image. A man came up to the house . . . for a week, an artist I mean, and painted a picture of Daddy. It was painted in a definite style, a magazine cover style, and Daddy seemed to get himself mixed up with all the kings and presidents and so forth who had been on the cover before him. I mean he seemed in some way locked into the cover, fixed there, impressed on the paper. Once I lost my temper at him and said I don't think anybody's impressed by the fact that you had your face on *Time* magazine. . . . They have all kinds of people; broken down ball players and crooks. It hurt his feelings, you could see."

But the high spirits never lasted. As the sixties waned and the euphoria began to fade, my father discovered the real secret of success: it doesn't make any difference. No amount of money or adulation or Hollywood deals could diminish his depressions or his doubts. He was still alone. "He was a man who made his own world in relative isolation from most of his kind," my brother Fred wrote when I asked him to put down what he remembered about our father. "As a result he had to live with his own impulses and perceptions in ways that most of us can avoid. No one, absolutely no one shared his life with him. There was no one from whom he could get honest advice. Of course this state of affairs was very much his own doing, but it must have been hard sometimes."

In many ways my father's life can be divided into two distinct parts. The first forty-five years or so were devoted to a struggle for stability: the establishment of a professional reputation, the creation of a family, earning enough money to survive, and most of all the search for some kind of home — some place of his own that might confirm his credentials as a gentleman and soothe his insecurities. The last twenty years of my father's life were spent in a struggle to escape the trappings and traps he had so carefully constructed for himself: to free himself from marriage and the legal and emotional constraints of the conventional upper-middle-class life, to leave behind the torpid stability of the suburbs and the responsibilities of a house and family, and most of all to escape the pressure to continually surpass himself as a writer.

"My incantation has changed," he wrote in 1969 after *Bullet Park* had been panned by the critics and his alcoholism was worse and most of the money was spent. "I am no longer sitting under an apple tree in clean chinos reading. I am sitting naked in the yellow chair in the dining room. In my hand there is a large crystal glass filled to the brim with honey colored whiskey. There are two ice cubes in the whiskey. I am smoking six or seven cigarettes and thinking contentedly about my interesting travels in Egypt and Russia. When the glass is empty I fill it again with ice and whiskey and light another cigarette although there are several burning in the ashtray. I am sitting naked in a yellow chair drinking whiskey and smoking six or seven cigarettes."

My father tried various ways to ease his situation, or to escape it. He tried drinking, he tried love affairs, and he tried travel. For the first time in his life he had the money to go wherever he wanted, and as his fame increased, invitations came from magazines and governments and universities all over the world. My father went almost everywhere. He still suffered horribly from vertigo and anxiety, but he was able to suppress his fears in order to see the world that until then he had only been able to dream about. Travel was escape and education at once, and he also found it exceedingly pleasant to be given the red-carpet treatment that some governments and organizations proffer distinguished visitors. There was nothing like a deferential butler passing drinks on a silver tray, or a pretty interpreter, or a blonde ambassador's wife gushing about his work, to make him feel that he was home at last.

In 1965, after returning from Russia, he spent a few months in Rome at the invitation of the American Academy. Then in the winter of 1967 he took my mother and brother to Curaçao, and in the summer the three of them spent two weeks in Naples, where my father wrote a piece on Sophia Loren for *Look* magazine. In the winter of 1968 we all went back to Curaçao, and the next spring he and my mother and Fred went to Ireland for a month. In 1969 we were all in Spain for the summer, and in 1970 he took my mother and Fred to Japan, and to Korea for the International P.E.N. Congress. That fall he took Fred to Russia. He also went to Cairo, to Venezuela, and back and forth to Rome and London several times during these years. Travel was sometimes uncomfortable and sometimes exhilarating.

As he had been fascinated by Italy and the Italians in the 1950s, my father became fascinated by Russia and the Russians. "We go to the Bolshoi for one of those old fashioned vaudeville performances. An orchestra, a recitation, a mezzo soprano. I nearly fall asleep," he wrote during his second trip to Russia. "Waking before dawn I have the travelers blues. If there is a knock at the door shall I jump out of the window? There are no exits, fire escapes or stairs in the [Hotel] Ukraine and in case of fire we will roast. I drink vodka for breakfast and we fly to Tbilisi. The first feast is with a family and all the toasts stress this. The oldest man is toasted first, then the youngest. I find this very moving. The next feast is in the mountains near the Turkish border. . . . Geese, pigs, cows and sheep wander over the road. The bus collides with a bull. We come to the center of the province, a place of the most outstanding bleakness. This is what Russian literature, Russian song is about. In the distance are the mountains covered with snow. It is dusk in the corridors of the central committee. The clocks are broken. The toilet is smeared with shit and urine. In the main square there is a statue of Lenin and there is a cow. So we drive up into the mountains for our feast."

My father loved Russia for her contrasts, for the old-fashioned agricultural society and customs he saw there, for the alcoholic friendliness of the people, for the way he was feted and loved, and also because it was so far away. He went to Russia three times and to Eastern Europe twice; his attraction for these places seemed so strong that we used to joke that he was going to be the first western writer to defect to the East. He told dozens of stories — stories about Russia and Rumania and Bulgaria; about a soothsayer he had seen in the mountains; about seeing the paintings in the Hermitage in Leningrad; about a man who shared his lunch with an old woman on a boat in the Danube; about his friends Yevtushenko and Tanya Litvinov; and about the Byzantine politics of the writers' union in Moscow. He loved to tell people that the only serious fight he had had with his son Fred was over whether or not they could visit the cruiser *Aurora* when they were in Leningrad.

My brother Fred describes their Russian trip this way: "On the ground in the Soviet Union we were taken around in Cheka limos, a cross between a barn and a Checker cab, usually carpeted in the back with scraps of Persian rug. Come to think of it, I think Dad was more in love with the idea of traveling than he was with the actuality. As I remember, he did not find experiencing new places exhilarating. I remember going to Leningrad with him. I wanted to see the *Aurora* which was docked across the river from our hotel. He did not, and he made that quite clear. We ended up walking down the Nevsky Prospekt to the Winter Palace and then turning around. I think that like many people in the Soviet Union he was always a little afraid that they were going to kidnap him, as a result he always said very nice things when asked about their country."

My father traveled because he couldn't stay at home, and, like Hammer in *Bullet Park*, to escape his "cafard" — that existential dread for which the best antidote was his work. Travel was always interesting, and the trips we took as a family were fun because of the pleasure my father took in playing the role of provider and interpreter of experience. But I think my father was also looking for something more spiritual, a confirmation of his own belief in the importance of transcendence and the vitality of the soul. Perhaps he expected that some landscape encountered at the turn of the road high up in the mountains near Turkey, or some peasant's face as he stood in his fields and watched the limousine go by, or some Italian princess floating through her drawing rooms, would provide a crucial moment of enlightenment for him — a turn of the key.

In the meantime, even the house in Ossining didn't seem much like home, he complained in his journal after an argument with my mother. "I have turned and fertilized every foot of soil but my wife has preempted the place and I am homeless," he wrote. "Then I think of feeling myself an expatriate in Venezuela sitting on the terrace of the Diazes. So perhaps my sense of home will never be established. To acquiesce to the role of a wanderer seems to be compromising."

✳   ✳   ✳

In 1962 my mother had been recruited for a part-time job teaching English at Briarcliff College, a few minutes' drive from the Ossining house. It was the first salaried job she had had since I was born, and it gave her a new kind of confidence. She was a gifted teacher, and the job became terribly important to her. The girls at Briarcliff were famous for their carefree good looks; this seemed to rub off on my mother. At the age of forty-five she blossomed, becoming more beautiful than she had been as a girl. She shed her stodgy matronly clothes for bright silks and expensive leather, and she had her hair done and began taking care of her skin. Her body slimmed and elongated from yoga classes, and her posture went from a slump to a swinging, effortlessly graceful walk. She loved to look in the mirror. But my mother's teaching and her confidence put a new strain on the marriage. As she became more interested in herself and her own world, she became less interested in my father. Teaching revived her own creative ambitions, and she began to write the tough, lyrical poems that were later collected in *The Need for Chocolate*. The potential irony of his wife losing interest in him because she was teaching creative writing to a bunch of gorgeous bubbleheads was not lost on my father. My parents' arguments became worse. He was more and more sarcastic, she was often angry and cold.

In the late 1960s, after Hope Lange and Alan Pakula were divorced, Hope and my father began an affair that continued on and off for the rest of his life. I think my father loved Hope, but their friendship was very sporadic. She lived in Los Angeles, which he rarely visited, and even when she was staying in New York he liked to catch the early train home to Ossining. Hope says that she loved my father, but that she never would have wanted to live with him. She accepted the permanence of his marriage, and she met my mother at screenings and readings that my father had asked them both to attend. My father knew that Hope was not really available, but that didn't keep him from daydreaming.

By 1969, when we all spent the summer in Deyá, a small town on the coast of Majorca, the financial and critical success that had seemed so well deserved had already begun to evaporate. His third novel, *Bullet Park*, had not had the critical or popular response his reputation now required, and he wasn't working on anything else. He was sick often, and the winter before he had broken his leg while skiing in the orchard. His face and body were bloated from drinking too much, and he still limped. In 1969 he felt rich, and our summer in Spain included side trips to Rome and Madrid, all first class; by 1970 he was poor again. The benevolence with which he had urged us to spend money in the past was soon to be replaced by angry accusations of improvidence. Six months after we parted in Spain, ending a trip that must have cost more than $10,000, I asked him for a $200 loan to help buy a secondhand car. Nothing doing. The money was gone.

The euphoria we had all felt in the 1960s made the disasters of the early 1970s harder to bear. There was more

pressure on my father, who had taken on financial obligations and a style of living that he now felt he had to keep
up. He also had literary critics to contend with; during this
time some critics took the line that he had been a good
writer but that his career was over — a particularly galling
assessment. My mother's job became a financial as well as
emotional strain, he claimed, because her salary was just
enough to put them in a higher tax bracket.

It became clearer and clearer that my father was the worst
kind of alcoholic. He seemed intent on destroying himself.
I suppose he had always been an alcoholic. Even in the
army he spent his free evenings down at Willie's Bar in
Augusta, Georgia, and his favorite luxury was a pint of
whiskey of his own for private pulls when he got low. For
years he had been proud of his ability to imbibe large
amounts of hard liquor. In those days, drinking was a manly
indulgence, a confirmation of power and courage and masculine endurance. All great writers drank. My father's friendships were all drinking friendships. He emptied martini
shakers with Winter and Polly at Treetops, downed three
stiff ones before lunch with Phil Boyer every weekend morning that we lived in Scarborough, and drowned dozens of
afternoons in Zinny Schoales's living room at Beechwood
sipping from her outsized glasses with the VVS monograms.
There were preprandial libations, as Zinny called them, and
postprandial libations, and soon there were libations all the
time. My father's focus on liquor was so intense that he
judged people primarily by how much they drank and by
the strength of the drinks they served him. When he came
back from a visit to F. Scott Fitzgerald's daughter in George-
town, I remember him explaining how much he liked her —
especially because of the robustness of the drinks she served,
which seemed, the way he told it, to reflect an excellence of

character. For him, hospitality meant offering each guest in his house a drink the moment they stepped through the door and then mixing whatever they asked for in proportions that would have knocked out an elephant. He was proud of the fact that he had made his father's first martini cocktail — and that the old gent had said it was "strong enough to draw a boat." Friends and interviewers often left my father's house in a happy daze, convinced that they had been unusually witty and charming.

In the 1960s two things changed almost simultaneously. My father began to need more liquor to make him feel satisfactorily high, and his body began to tolerate it less. At about 10:30 A.M. he would come downstairs from the room where he was working and sit in the yellow wing chair in the living room and read and chain-smoke Marlboros. The pantry, with its row of gin and whiskey bottles and cabinet of glasses and its rarely used silver ice bucket, was a few feet away. As noon approached my father became irritable and impatient. It was a good time to stay away from him.

"Back at the house I want a drink," he wrote, describing a Sunday morning before a party at John and Barbara Hersey's house in Connecticut. "Nine o'clock. I read the *Times* book review section and the magazine. Mary is in the kitchen with a clear view of the bourbon bottle. The beds are unmade I know, but she lingers in the kitchen. Then she goes outside to sweep the porch but should I make a grab for the bourbon I might be seen through the pantry window. I hope she will go into the garden and pick some flowers but she does not. She returns to the dining room and rearranges some ashtrays. I go on reading the *Times*. Then she starts up the stairs but changes her mind and returns to the kitchen. Finally she climbs the stairs to the first landing and then the second and I sail into the pantry and gulp down two hookers of bourbon. At half past eleven I get out the ice and settle down to formal drinking. I need the drinks to make the drive to Connecticut."

Often when he seemed sulky or displeased, my father was just busy calculating our movements in relation to sneaking his next drink. Although none of us ever policed his drinking — in fact we rarely even mentioned it — part of my father's addiction to alcohol seemed to involve a need for secrecy. He had to be getting away with something. No one could know. There were always bottles of gin and whiskey on full view in the pantry, but he also kept a bottle in his closet, a bottle in the desk where he worked, a bottle behind the New York Edition of Henry James in the library, and, in warm weather, a bottle outside in the hedge near the driveway.

As the months went by in the last years of the 1960s and the first years of the 1970s, the inevitable first drink of the day came sooner and sooner. Eventually it blended with the last drink of the evening, or the drink at midnight or three in the morning so he could get back to sleep. There was always an excuse. He needed the drink to drive to New York or to the liquor store, or he needed it to sleep, or he needed it to get through a party my mother was dragging him to, or he needed it to dull the disappointment he felt in his children, or he needed it to work.

My father forestalled any criticism of his drinking habits by frequently criticizing himself. He freely admitted that he was drinking too much, but he made no real move to stop. There were times, though, when he seemed willing to do anything else *but* stop, and so in the 1960s he started seeing local psychiatrists to discuss his drinking problem. My father didn't like psychiatrists or psychiatry. His fear that he was no more than the sum of the tawdry images of his past was expressed in a scorn for Freudian investigation. For him, the possibility of discounting his childhood experiences was a matter of great consequence. He had spent his life escaping the past; he wasn't about to return voluntarily. He felt that he understood the power of Freud's writings (although he never made any distinction between psychiatry and psychoanalysis) and rejected it. "The acceptance, the enthusiastic reception of Freudian thought and the vehemence with which it was then attacked," he wrote in his journal, "display how most of us are deeply convinced that given some turn of the key — an interpretation of dreams or a clarification of carnal love — we can all begin to lead more useful lives."

His first complaint about every psychiatrist was that the psychiatrist hadn't read his work. How could they understand him if they hadn't read his work? Most of them hadn't read much of anything, and certainly not *Les Faux Monnayeurs* or *Il Gattopardo* or Goncharov or even Fielding. How could he be expected to communicate with men like that?

His second complaint was that the psychiatrists always wanted to talk about his mother. They told him that he hated women. Had anyone ever heard of anything so ridiculous? Just this week he had had another love letter from Hope or Ellen or Nancy. They told him that his feelings were traceable to his childhood. He didn't see how the fact that his mother ran a gift shop could be responsible for his urge to drink before noon.

But urged by our family doctor and his family, he dutifully went off to Dr. X, who practiced in the basement of a Victorian mansion on the hill in Tarrytown, and then to Dr. Y, who had an office crowded with tricycles and basketballs that he used in working with children, and then to

Dr. Z, who smoked a pipe and recommended that my father eat more bran.

When he was at Phelps Memorial Hospital after his first heart attack, another psychiatrist came to talk with him. He was young, with elaborately blown-dry hair and boots with side zippers. My father called him "The Boots." A few months after my father got out of the hospital, the family doctor called me to talk about my father. He had started drinking again, and we were all extremely concerned.

"You know, Susie, your father really *hates* psychiatrists," he said.

"Tell me about it."

"You'll never guess what he told that young doctor who saw him in the hospital."

"I don't know, something ridiculous?" I said. "He doesn't trust them."

"He told that one he was homosexual!" The doctor laughed at this new example of my father's intransigence. "Can you beat that?"

Later on I called my father. I thought his attitude toward psychiatrists was silly.

"Come on, Daddy," I said. "Why did you go and tell 'The Boots' that you were homosexual?"

There was a little silence on the line, and then my father laughed too. "I guess I just don't like psychiatrists," he said.

Seventeen

My grandfather Cheever was not a religious man, but he liked to attend Sunday services at the Unitarian church and sit with the bankers and other prosperous local merchants. My grandmother started life as an Anglican, and her family became Episcopalian when they immigrated to Boston. She too was Episcopalian in the years before she embraced the teachings of Mrs. Mary Baker Eddy, and she had her infant son christened John William in the Episcopal church in Quincy. Later, the family stopped going to church entirely, but the resonance of Bishop Thomas Cranmer's services in the old Book of Common Prayer had made a permanent impression on my father's prose style and on his view of the world. He began going to church again in New York in the 1930s, when he fell in love for the first time and "realized the number of imponderables in my life," he told me once. "Ecstasy was much more mysterious to me than grief."

When I was a child my father took me to church at St. Thomas's in New York, and later to St. Mary's across Route

9 from Beechwood in Scarborough and to All Saints on the corner of Briarcliff Road, ensuring that I would be impressed with the sonorous phrasing of Cranmer's litany. "Come unto me all ye that travail and are heavy laden, and I will refresh you." I hated Sunday school, but I loved church — the mysterious glittering figures at the altar, the light as it filtered through the stained-glass scene of the Virgin with her child asleep in a manger, Cranmer's robust, comforting prayers and confession, and most of all the sense that there was something beyond the miserable details of everyday life. In 1955 my father was confirmed at All Saints, an act that reflected a mixture of gratitude and hope. After that he and I went to early communion there when we were in Scarborough, and to other churches wherever we were — Nantucket, Rome, New Hampshire. I remember the combination of enthusiasm and reluctance I felt on many of those early mornings, and the dampness in the church that gave me what he called "the ecclesiastical sniffles." Even in church my father's powers of observation were never suspended, and he couldn't resist cracking away at the parochial ambitions of the dwindling small-town parishes. I think he hoped to find at church some sense of redemption for the sins he had committed by thought, word, and deed against what he saw as the purity and innocence of the natural world — a world somehow represented by Christianity. The orderly patterns of ecclesiastical ritual were another bulwark against the chaos of his conflicts and desires. It wasn't simple.

"Easter. Dressing for church the iconography seems more than ever threadbare," he wrote in 1965. "The maidenly cross, the funeral lily, the lavender bow pulled off a candy box. How poorly this serves the catechism of the resurrection. All the candles burn. Miss E. has worked night and day on the flower arrangements. The organist, truly raised from the dead, improvises a sort of polymorphous fugue. We raise our voices in some tuneless doggerel about life everlasting. These are earnest people, mostly old, making an organized response to the mysteriousness of life. I hope, I go not further, to avoid anger, meanness, sloth; to be manly and should I be unable to mend my affairs, to act with common sense."

Journalists have written that my father went to church every Sunday but that he invariably stepped out during the sermon to smoke a cigarette. This has a nice ring, but it's wrong on two counts. First, my father was a supremely courteous man and would never have stood up and left a church in the middle of a service. Second, he never ever went to the 11 A.M. Morning Worship service, where the sermon is preached. Instead he went to the 8 A.M. Early Communion service, where there is no sermon — he had clocked this service at thirty-three minutes flat. His religious requirements — that the service come from Cranmer's rites in the old prayer book, that it take thirty-three minutes or less, that the church be within ten minutes' driving distance, and that the altar be sufficiently simple so that it wouldn't remind him of a gift shop — limited his choice of parishes. While we lived in Scarborough, he went to All Saints, where the minister, William Arnold, was an old friend of my father's friend Arthur Spear, a fellow parishioner. Bill Arnold even bought one of our Labrador puppies, a son of Cassiopeia, and this friendly canine sometimes appeared smiling and snuffling on the other side of the communion rail as we knelt there to receive the most precious body and blood of Our Lord Jesus Christ.

After my parents had moved north to Ossining, my father began going to Trinity Church, a gray stone pile at the top of Main Street that was closer to home than All Saints. As a regular churchgoer and a prosperous resident with a growing reputation, my father became a kind of local celebrity. And in 1970, he sought out Father George Kandel, the chaplain of the Ossining Correctional Facility, to talk about the possibility of teaching a course in writing to the inmates. The Ossining Correctional Facility, more generally known as Sing Sing, or the Prison, had been a fact of life for us since we settled in Scarborough. When I was a child, it would thrill me to be driven down through the first gates and along the high, impenetrable outer walls. From the railroad tracks along the river where we used to play, we could see the dramatic silhouettes of the guard towers and the armed guards atop the great cell-block wall. Sometimes I would drive up Revolutionary Road to the parking lot of the abandoned Ossining Hospital to look down at the main building with its high windows and endless corridors. There was a fascination in confinement, a fascination in all those lives being lived so close to us and yet so very differently.

In 1971 my father entered the locked doors of the prison administration building, was escorted in a bus around the perimeter of the yard, and went through the locked doors of the education building to get to his first class. There were about thirty students gathered to hear him, more than half of them were black or Hispanic, and a lot of them had just come to argue. The prison was a frightening place. My father was teaching during the Attica prison riots upstate, and his students kept telling him that he would make a great hostage. But the excitement of introducing ignorant men to the power of literature and watching their spontaneous reaction was also overwhelming. The students who kept coming to class had a responsiveness and concentration unknown in the world outside. Some of them started to write their own stories, and a few of them wrote well. Their language was crude and their responses wildly unconventional. My father knew he wanted to teach them when one Chicano student with the body of a weight lifter raised his hand in a discussion on power and stood up to speak. "Oh, what a cooool motherfucker was that Machiavelli," he said, and then he let out a low whistle, nodded appreciatively, and sat down.

My father identified with the prisoners. Like them he was at once guilty and innocent, like them he was outside society, like them he was trapped, confined — but by nothing as simple as armed guards and iron bars. His closest friendship at the prison was with Donald Lang, a pale, lanky thirty-one-year-old who had served half his life in jail for armed robbery. Lang delighted my father with a lively, raunchy satire entitled "The Pit-Wig Papers," ostensibly about a plan to sell hairpieces for underarm use. About a year after my father started teaching at Sing Sing, Lang was paroled — he already had been in and out three times — and sent to a halfway house in Poughkeepsie. My father drove down Main Street to the prison to get him.

"I see Donald out. But before this I see him half awake. A cadaverous young man, not quite a runt. His pallor is luminous," he wrote in his journal. "The morning is beautiful but so cold that the beauty misses me although I know it to be there. Spotty and moving lights. Snow on the mountains. I had imagined the scene to be highly emotional, embraces, perhaps tears. I see him for the first time out of prison uniform. He has a dark suit, a dark raincoat, Italian shoes and a string tie. All this darkness makes him seem more cadaverous. There are no emotional excesses. Smiles and firm handshakes. The splendor of the river on a cold day. He walks out of the prison in which he has spent half his life. These [prison] bars are an incarnation not of our society, but of our world's inability to produce a workable concept of justice and penance. Here are the bars, clangorous, needing paint, the facts of our sense of good and evil, arbitrary, vestigial, and cruel."

It was the day he went to pick up Lang that my father noticed the way the white paint was worn off the bars at just the height where a man would put his hands if he was standing and waiting for something. Lang stayed in Poughkeepsie for a while, and later he came back to Ossining to live with some friends of my parents. He's been in some trouble, but he hasn't been back in jail. My father lent him money, gave him jobs around the house (he turned out to be an expert carpenter), and bought him a car. In return, Lang sat down afternoon after afternoon and told my father everything he remembered about the prison: the way the guards were called assholes and the way they acted to get that name; the sexual codes and the drugs and the violence and the way one of the assholes killed a prisoner's pet cat with a club one day.

"I started out as a 'fucking do-gooder,' as the guards used to call me, one particular guard who had a shaved head," my father told me years later when he had written a novel about a prison called *Falconer*. "And then it wasn't until about a year after I'd been there that what is the blasphemy, what is the true horror of prison, which is the imponderable that I've tried to put in the book, came to me. The blasphemy of men creating and building stone by stone hells for other men. This is still an indescribable horror. After that I went there very unwillingly. It seemed to me to be participating in an obscenity."

My father lasted as a teacher at Sing Sing for a little more than a year. But his experience at the prison gave him the symbols and the facts to use in writing about his own sense of confinement and entrapment.

The prison had another important effect, I think. For decades my father had been wrestling with his own lusts. He found his desires unacceptable — and so did the society he lived in. When, occasionally, he was overpowered by the force of his instincts, he paid for his pleasure with agonizing periods of guilt. He had betrayed his family, he had betrayed himself, he had betrayed the laws of society. Teaching at Sing Sing made him think again about the wisdom of those laws.

Eighteen

"Having nothing better to do — which is a mistaken position to have gotten into — I read two old journals," my father wrote in 1967 at the height of his first success. "High spirits and weather reports recede in the background and what emerges are two astonishing contests, one with alcohol and one with my wife. With alcohol I record my failures, but the number of mornings when I've sneaked drinks in the pantry is appalling. As for the marriage a number of things appear. The useful is a view of marriage that is neither larky nor desperate, a sense of how large a continent it is and how complex are its burdens. Sentiment and intelligence seem more important than passion. There are many accounts of sexual and romantic ecstasy, but they are outnumbered by an incredible number of rebuffs."

There was a third contest in my father's life; a contest so intense and so secret that he kept all but oblique mentions of it out of his journals for decades; a contest that dominates his journal entries in the 1970s and 1980s and that was probably linked to his battles with alcohol and with my mother. My father's awareness of this contest began earlier than his awareness of the others — with the adolescent games played with his brother and other Quincy boys, and with his parents' tactlessly expressed fear that their runty, unathletic younger son John was somehow less than manly. It lasted long after the others were resolved, too; long after my father had given up drinking and come to a truce with my mother.

My father's sexual appetites were one of his major preoccupations, and his lust for men was as distressing to him as his desire for women was self-affirming and ecstatic. The journals contain argument after argument with himself on the subject of homosexuality. Although he loved men, he feared and despised what he defined as the homosexual community; the limp-wristed, lisping men who are sometimes the self-appointed representatives of homosexual love in our culture. Men who run gift shops, sell antiques, strike bargains over porcelain tea sets. He was terrified that his enjoyment of homosexual love would estrange him from the natural world, from the pure and anchoring influence of his family, from the manly pleasures he also loved. He had been brought up in a world and in a religion that rejected homosexuality absolutely.

"I read a biography of Tolstoy," he wrote in 1968 after finishing Henri Troyat's *Tolstoy*. "It is mentioned in passing that he loved men as well as women — a telling remark for me. It is a dangerously eccentric society that intends to regulate sentimental and erotic love. I wish I could speak clearly about these dark matters. I did not respond consciously to the anxiety my parents endured over the possibility that I might be a pervert, but I seem to have responded at some other level. I can't really blame them since they had no way of improvising sexual mores but had they been less anxious,

less suspicious about my merry games of grabarse I might
have had an easier life. But what is done is done and cannot
be undone at an hour a minute in the office of Dr. Doheny.
How inestimable is the cruelty of sexual legislation."

Sometimes my father blamed his parents. Their fear of
homosexuality was so great — their emphasis on the separation of sexual roles so rigid — that his own ambivalence
was ordained. Sometimes he blamed my mother. When she
wouldn't give him the sexual and emotional love he needed
— and she often didn't — he was forced to turn elsewhere.
Other times he blamed society, arguing over and over that
the preindustrial world that had required the undistracted
cooperation of men and women to raise crops and breed
children was now outdated, but that laws and society's judg-
ment had failed to change accordingly.

"My uninformed feeling has been that in agricultural
and maritime societies homosexuality is self-destructive,"
he wrote. "In the past agriculture depended upon a steadily
increasing population and in the maritime world of my
grandfather the long sailing voyages made any sentimental
and erotic liaisons suicidal. And there do seem to have been
periods in time when we have enjoyed a forthright robustness that allowed us to see the depth and beauty of the love
men feel for one another but within the framework of pro-
creative love rather or exactly as if this were the force of
gravity. The vastness of this anxiety is something that I
have not seen put down."

My father had had his share of heterosexual affairs, but
when he began to give in to his love for other men, he was
more confused and self-condemning than he had ever been.
The sexual freedom of the 1960s made matters worse. He
had spent fifty years suppressing his homosexual longings
and his bawdy obsession with sex in all its forms. Now

all around him other writers were coming out of the closet. John Rechy's *City of Night* and James Baldwin's *Giovanni's Room* were just two of the novels dealing specifically and graphically with homosexual life. I think this made him even more determined to keep his secret. For decades he carefully expunged any frank or scatological language from his prose to satisfy the requirements of *The New Yorker* and publishing-house editors. In a way, his natural reticence made him feel that they were right — at least in some cases. When *The Wapshot Chronicle* was published in 1957, when I was thirteen, he asked me not to read it; and when the paperback was issued with a vaguely suggestive cover, a frieze of men and women intertwined, he tore off the covers of all the copies that came into the house. But suddenly, in the 1960s, his respected contemporaries, as well as everyone else, were publishing descriptions that would have been unthinkable and unprintable for most of his career.

"Great progress in this kind of writing has been made in the last few years while I persevere in trying to write a novel without a four letter word," he complained in 1968. "Donleavy, Mailer, Roth, Updike, some of the most important men we have are writing about cocks and cunts and arseholes while I describe the summer dawn."

I think it was partly his fear of his own desires that kept my father drinking, and I think his anxiety over his sexual ambivalence also kept him married. As long as he was the Ossining squire, the father of three, the dog-loving, horseback riding, meadow-scything, long-suffering husband, there could be no doubt in the public mind about his sexual preferences, and perhaps less doubt in his own. After his heart attacks and his alcoholic collapse and his decision to live, he seemed to come to better terms with himself. *Fal-*

coner, the novel he wrote after he stopped drinking in 1975, is peppered with scatological language and centers on a tender and larky homosexual love.

For those who wished to look for them, there were clues to his sexual nature everywhere. Coverly Wapshot struggles furiously with his sexual confusion, his disturbing attraction to other men, and homosexual men's assumption that he is one of them. The short stories often deal with close male and homosexual relationships. In the last decade of his life, my father became close to a series of younger male "protégés," some of them quite overtly homosexual. Still, few people really guessed. The image he cultivated of a patrician, old-fashioned country gentleman must have been very convincing. He didn't want us to know — and we didn't want to know.

※　　※　　※

I remember once about ten years ago walking through the pantry of my parents' house early in the afternoon. There was a letter lying open and out of its envelope on the shelf under the cabinet where the glasses are kept. Idly, half out of boredom, I unfolded it and saw that it was a note from Captain Dennis Coates, an army officer and a teacher at West Point who was writing his dissertation on my father's novels. Denny had spent several weekends with my father, enough time to become a family friend, and he had even named his cocker spaniel puppy Cheever. It was a nice letter, delicate and polite, explaining that although he was very fond of my father, he could not accept his physical affection. I folded the letter back up and wandered idly into the kitchen. The odd thing is this: Although I have always remembered reading that letter — the way the light slanted through the small windowpanes, the musty smell of the pantry sink — it wasn't until after my father died and I read his journals that I remembered what the letter meant.

"Talk about innocence!" Denny Coates said when I located him at the Armed Forces Staff College in Norfolk, Virginia, where he is a lieutenant colonel now. "I went over there one Sunday afternoon and your father said to me, 'I've just finished a story. I want to read it to you,' and it was 'The Leaves, the Lionfish and the Bear.' So we sat there at the dining room table and he read it to me and he held my hand. I was thrilled because I loved the story and I thought, Well, I'm probably the first person alive to hear this. Later on we took a walk. He liked me. He just said 'Hold me,' and I did. I thought maybe he was cold. But what he wanted was sex. So I had to say I couldn't do that. I knew it was love for him. He said he knew nothing about technique. For him it was a matter of love. After that incident we became more reserved and formal with each other."

Nineteen

ALTHOUGH MY FATHER WAS never particularly popular with reviewers, until the end of his life, *The Wapshot Chronicle* got predictable first-novel praise from some critics (quite a few suggested that he stick to short stories), and it won the National Book Award. *The Wapshot Scandal* also received mixed but fairly respectful reviews (and more suggestions that he stick to the short story), as did the collections of stories that appeared in the late 1950s and early 1960s. But it was in the mid-1960s that my father's reputation really began to soar, with the *Time* cover, the Howells Medal, and the movie sales. There were, therefore, very high expectations all around for his third novel, *Bullet Park*, which was published by Knopf in April of 1969. Not only was it the first novel in five years from a writer who had become famous, established, and respected during that time but it was an important book, an ambitious book, a long rich story with lots of characters, suburban texture combined with strong narrative, and a metaphysical theme that made it clear that the story was about a good deal more than the

daily commute, PTA meetings, lost cats, and the local Episcopal church.

Hopes got higher as word came that the *New York Times
Book Review* was devoting its entire front page to *Bullet
Park*. Christopher Lehmann-Haupt had done a wonderful
interview with my father that we heard was to appear on
page 2 of the *Book Review*. I'll never forget the afternoon
Candida Donadio, my father's agent, called to report that
the interview had been bumped to the back pages. My father
knew it was a favorable interview, and he knew right away
that something was wrong. It was a warm, late-winter day
and there were blossoms at the top of the star magnolia tree
that grows beside the brook below the orchard. We went
outside and sat in the sun on the porch. My father seemed
suddenly very frail.

The review was unfavorable, and to my father, the reviewer seemed to be saying that his career was over, his
talent was shot. It was certainly a bad review, but my
father's reaction to it was even worse. What hurt him most,
I think, was the reviewer's praise for the stories coupled
with his complete failure to recognize the ambition and
energy and vision *Bullet Park* embodied — whether or not
it was successful. Two days after the Sunday review, John
Leonard wrote a respectful but very low-key review in the
daily *New York Times*. Under the circumstances, Knopf did
not invest heavily in advertising, and *Bullet Park* eventually
sold 33,000 copies, a barely respectable minimum for a man
with my father's reputation. It didn't recoup the advance, it
won no prizes, it was quickly forgotten.

My father's instinctive feeling was that he never wanted
to publish again, and he almost didn't. In 1972 Candida
Donadio and Robert Gottlieb at Knopf persuaded him to
publish a slim collection of the ten short stories he had eked

Above: Cheever eats an apple while Labrador Flora Macdonald hungrily looks on.
Below: At work in Susan's bedroom in Ossining.

rry Benson

Above: In a Russian audience with the poet Yevtushenko in 1964. *Below:* At Brown University to give a speech while Susan was a student there.

Brown Daily Herald

Nancy Crampton

© 1982 Thomas Victor

Above, left: Mary Cheever with Ben Cheever at the National Book Critics Circle award ceremony. *Above, right:* With Fred Cheever. *Below:* Receiving an honorary degree at Harvard University in June of 1978. *Overleaf:* John Cheever.

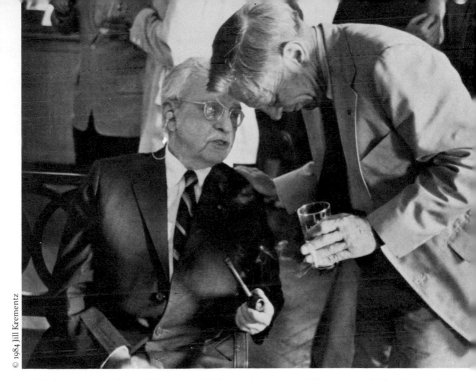

© 1984 Jill Krementz

The years after the publication of *Falconer* in 1977 and *The Stories of John Cheever* in 1978 were a time of recognition and honors. *Above:* With Malcolm Cowley in 1977 at the annual award ceremony of the American Academy of Arts and Letters. *Below:* With Saul Bellow and Dick Cavett at the National Arts Club in 1978.

© 1982 Thomas Vic

Above: John Cheever, Mary Cheever, Susan Cheever, Flora, and Maisie on the terrace in Ossining. *Below:* Playing backgammon with Arthur Spear in the dining room.

© Nancy Crampton

© Nancy Crampton

© Edgar Stillman
© Nancy Crampto

Above: Reading "The Pit-Wig Papers," written by Donald Lang *(right)* in Cheever's writing class at Sing Sing Prison. *Below:* Yevtushenko, John Cheever, and John Updike.

© Nancy Crampton

Harry Benson

 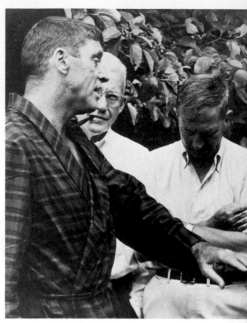

Above, left: The Cheevers on the lawn in Ossining. *Above, right:* Burt Lancaster, Arthur Spear, and John Cheever on the set of the movie *The Swimmer* in Westport, Connecticut. *Below:* Cheever in the empty swimming pool at Beechwood.

arry Benson

out during the 1960s, in between novels, traveling, and alcoholic interludes. Many of the stories had been rejected by *The New Yorker*, and six of the ten had appeared in *Esquire*, *The Saturday Evening Post*, or *Playboy*. Although some of them are wonderful, others suggest financial desperation and the alcoholic lack of concentration that seeped into my father's work at the end of the decade. In light of what had happened to *Bullet Park*, it seemed sad and ironic that *The World of Apples*, as the collection was called, was widely praised by the critics. This time the *New York Times Book Review* devoted its front page to a rave review. I remember that day too. The Sunday morning in 1973 that the review appeared, I took it to Phelps Memorial Hospital to show my father. He had just had his first heart attack, and he was hallucinating that he was in a Russian prison camp. He thought the review was a confession that he was being asked to sign, and he swore at me and threw it on the floor. The nurse came over and took it away.

❋   ❋   ❋

Of course the critics didn't cause the collapse of my father's health and fortunes — if anything, they just chronicled it. My father had taken a large advance from Knopf for his novel about a prison, which turned out to be *Falconer*. The money was spent and the novel barely started. He was drinking heavily and taking various combinations of Valium, Librium, and Seconal to keep himself from drinking even more. At the same time that he was obliterating his intelligence with drink and drugs and wiping out the last of his bank balance, his marriage continued to get worse. Everything got worse.

"Yesterday my hands shook so that I could not type," he wrote a year after *Bullet Park* came out.

In the morning I drink half a bottle of Courvoisier there being nothing else in the house. In the afternoon I drink more than half a bottle of Bushmills. This morning — a brilliant day for the first time in weeks — things are better but I suffer from a slight psychological double vision — a melancholy at the edge of my consciousness that has no discernible imagery. It is rather like a taste. I claim there is some connection between my need for drink and my need for love of some sort and I'm determined to put it down however clumsily.

This may be a neurotic condition, some injury done in my childhood. The situation has gone on for years. Mary responds periodically but then, in the twinkling of an eye and for no discernible reason we enter the gauls and barrens and stay there for months. I am not allowed a kiss; I am barely granted a good morning. This is acutely painful and is not I think the lot of every married man. There is the love I bear my children but this of course has its limitations. The need for love is a discernible form of nausea, an intestinal pain. I cure it by imagining I am with S. although I have not seen her for weeks.

My parents' marriage had always been characterized by periods of anger and silence, alternating with times when they seemed to rediscover each other and the possibilities of romantic love. In the early 1970s, as my father drank more and more and my mother developed her private life through a career, her poetry, and new friends, the periods of anger and silence between them increased. In July of 1971 my father was arrested by the state police in Somers, New York, for driving while intoxicated on the way home from a Saturday night dinner party at the Cowleys' house in Sherman, Connecticut. He had been crossing and recrossing the double yellow line, speeding down the wrong side of the road in the darkness. His license was suspended for sixty days, and he was fined seventy-five dollars. This, like his cast and crutches after the skiing accident, seemed a tangible

proof of how far he had fallen. Once he had been rich, successful, and loved by thousands of readers. Now he was poor
and very sick, a bloated old man with a funny accent trying
to talk his way out of a drunk-driving charge at a small-
town police station. A lot had happened in five years. He
blamed my mother bitterly for withholding her love from
him. This, he said, drove him to drink, to other women, to
despair. She blamed him for the family's financial situation,
for her own lack of freedom, and for a lot of other things.

When we children were at home during these years between 1969 and the mid-1970s, my parents would have
dinner together at the long table in front of the downstairs
fireplace as they always had, but they could rarely get
through the meal without a fight. She would leave the table
in tears, or he would get up in a cold, self-righteous rage.
His drinking had begun to have remarkable physical effects.
His speech slurred and his step was unsteady. Often after
he left the table we would hear him stamp and stumble up
the stairs and then there would be a series of crashes and
thuds as he tried to get down the narrow hall and up the
two steps into the bedroom. Both of my parents began to
talk a lot about other people in their lives — people who
understood them. They both confided at length and in ex-
plicit detail to me, or anyone else who would sit still long
enough to listen. Not only did I wish they wouldn't; I began
to wish they would get divorced. A tension seemed to be
building up between them that was almost intolerable —
certainly more intolerable than the wreck of their marriage,
the shattering of our family, and the sale of what we jok-
ingly referred to as "the ancestral homestead." The house
was at the center of things. My father had turned over the
soil, taken down dead trees, cleared the brush, and paid off
the mortgage. My mother had planned and nurtured the

flower gardens, furnished the rooms, fed the dogs, established her life and work there. Neither of them would leave. It came to seem a matter of angry stubbornness rather than of any kind of virtue.

※　　※　　※

When my father had his heart attack in 1973, my husband and I were staying with my parents (I had married Rob Cowley, Malcolm Cowley's son, in 1967), and my brother Fred was also living at home (in the fall he would go away to Andover). So it happened that when my father did collapse, the house was full of people who loved him and wanted him to live.

The afternoon before it happened, he had been mowing the big lawn and felt a searing pain across his chest. Naturally, he didn't mention it. He had a drink, and after a while he felt better. The next morning, though, he didn't get out of bed. He couldn't stop coughing. It was nothing, he assured us between long choking breaths, we shouldn't bother to call the doctor. Could someone get him another drink? I called the doctor, who suggested that we meet him at the Phelps Memorial emergency room as soon as possible. It took us almost an hour to get him out of bed and down to the car. First he had to have another cigarette, then he had to have another drink. Fred and I tried to ease him downstairs while my mother waited in the car. By the time she drove him up the driveway and out onto Route 9 the cough was uncontrollable.

He had had a major heart attack, the doctors said. The cough had been caused by his lungs filling up with fluid. In fact, he had almost died. They didn't want to give him the tranquilizing drugs that are usually given to alcoholics who go cold turkey, because his heart wasn't strong enough.

It was a delicate balance. For the first few days everything seemed calm as my father lay there breathing in and out through oxygen tubes. But on the third day he began to hallucinate. Left alone for a minute, he frantically detached the electrodes and tubes in order to escape the Russian prison guards. He had to be tied down. He thought the hospital food carts were truckloads of prisoners rumbling by outside the door. He thought the public-address-system speaker above his bed in the intensive care unit was a Bible that they wouldn't let him read. He was obsessed with escaping. Unguarded for a minute, he would pull out the tubes and wires that connected him to the heart monitor and the I.V. We took turns holding him down. When we fell asleep, they strapped him to the bed.

When my father came out of the hospital that time, he was chastened, apologetic, and very glad to be alive. He realized how much he had been drinking, he said; he was sorry for the pain and trouble he had caused. He would never drink again. And he did seem like a different man — as if being so close to death had given him a new life. His bloated body grew wiry. His jowly face became gaunt and his blue eyes seemed more prominent. Instead of moving clumsily through the house, bumping into things and falling down as he had before, he walked and sat with tremendous care and grace, as if he had suddenly become fragile and valuable. Instead of speaking in broad, bombastic, usually insulting terms, his voice was clipped and polite and appreciative. His recovery seemed to confirm his desire to live, and this gave him an air of youth and transcendent contentment. He had been through the fire.

It didn't last. My husband and I moved to New York, and my mother left for her annual summer stay at Treetops. Left alone in the house with my brother Fred, he began to slip.

First he claimed that the doctor had said he could have two drinks a day. Then he claimed that the doctor had said he could have a pint. A delegation of Japanese fans brought him a case of Suntory whiskey as a gift, and the bottles began to disappear from the box. When Fred noticed this, he dumped the rest of the whiskey down the pantry sink. I know now that alcoholism is a disease, not a failure of the will, and that the disease can never be cured, only arrested. But none of us knew that then.

My parents were still fighting when my mother returned from Treetops at the end of the summer, and my father left for the University of Iowa, where he had been invited to teach a semester at the Writers' Workshop. In Iowa his drinking steadily increased, but he still had the sense of having escaped death, and he had a wonderful time. He lived in a university hotel called Iowa House, and he went to the university football games and the museum and enjoyed the first academic community he had ever been a part of. He spent a lot of time with a then-little-known writer named John Irving, who shared his enthusiasm for Hemingway, football, and the joys of family life. Stranded on a midwestern campus, they referred to themselves as "closet easterners." "He made a great effort to take delight in things," says Irving, who was astonished by the jealousy and gossip that my father's presence engendered in the campus literary community. "He was not incapable of a nasty observation, but he was more capable of making it all right in the end. What you remembered was how much pleasure he took. He had the energy to be moved by every little thing." My father seemed undisturbed by his colleagues' envy, and he enjoyed the enthusiasm and adulation of his students. He was never alone. Specifically, he was never, or rarely, alone in bed. As his drinking began to take effect, the modicum of reticence my father had retained in discussing his adventures evaporated. When he came back from Iowa at Christmas, he talked endlessly about his heterosexual popularity: his affair with the photographer, his affair with the history professor, his affair with the adoring twenty-three-year-old student who still wrote him love letters every day. My father had discovered groupies.

His mood during this year of recovery and relapse at Iowa and in Ossining, as he drank more and worked on the prison novel that would not be finished until 1976, was alternately ecstatic and despairing. "Since I know so much about incarceration and addiction why can't I write about it?" he asked himself in the journal. "All I seem to be able to do is howl; let me out, let me out. What did I ever do to deserve this? I am both a prisoner and an addict." But a week later, at a different time of day, everything looked fine. "I am where I want to be," he wrote. "I sit at the window. I admire the beech and maple trees and the chestnut in bloom. Beyond the trees is the river and the hills or mountains. I think of C. Why do I love a girl with such a husky voice, I ask. She kisses me. Why do I love the oldest man in the world. Lang blows in the door. I can only stay a minute, he says, I'm double parked. He needs a bath."

A month later he was back in the doldrums: "Great days in their greatness, I seem to see the prison out of the corner of my eye. A spate of reviews in which I am thought to be charming and in which I am reminded to my shame of some cruelties in my work. I drink perhaps a tablespoon of whiskey — the first in three months. The effects are splendid, beyond anxiety. . . . I dine, watch a bad television show for my son's company and take the reviews out of the wastebasket to read them again."

Perhaps it was only a tablespoon of whiskey, but soon

after this entry, early in 1974, the journals stop almost completely. The few pages after this are badly typed, the place is not identified, and the prose is less than coherent.

❊   ❊   ❊

In the autumn of 1974 my father accepted an invitation to teach writing at Boston University. Although his condition was obviously deteriorating, he needed the money, and the atmosphere at home made anything else seem preferable. There's not much doubt that the fall and winter he spent teaching at B.U. and living in a furnished room off Kenmore Square, at 71 Bay State Road, was the lowest point in his life. Terrible things had happened to him in his adolescence — the loss of his home, the separation of his parents, the slide from prosperity to poverty. But Boston was worse. His drinking was completely out of control, and his incompetence began to seem suicidal. He thought he was going to die, and so did we.

My brother Fred, who was at school in nearby Andover, Massachusetts, that year, recalls this period as "a disaster in almost every possible way. He stopped eating but kept on drinking. Mom came up weekends as I remember and brought him food. His weakness made her very dutiful. I think I only came down from school two or three times. It was just too depressing. I had written him off at that point. I remember you telling me at Christmas that he was going to die. I also remember that this came as no great shock."

What coherent conversations my father was able to have during this time were usually sarcastic and cruel. Every exchange was characterized by accusations. It was because of our extravagance that he had been forced to go to Boston. It was because of my mother's coldness that he had

begun to drink again, and embarked on the series of affairs
that had become a family embarrassment. We stayed away
from him, and so did most people.

In Boston, he lunched with Gerald Brennan at Locke-
Ober and told everyone how his family had been lunching
there for generations. In faculty meetings, his colleague
Anne Sexton spiked his coffee with tiny bottles of liquor she
kept in her pocketbook. His brother Fred, who by that time
had lost his job at Pepperell and divorced his wife and was
living in a furnished room in Scituate, called him every day.
Fred was poor and out of work, but he had stopped drinking
and developed a sustaining group of friends. Once again he
began to take care of my father as he had when they were
boys, visiting as often as he could. Other people found
him harder to take.

"I'm sorry you weren't able to visit me here," he wrote
Denny Coates at West Point. "The classes remain spirited,
but this is scarcely a life. I divide my time between the
most disreputable hookers, the Harvard English Department
and the highest realms of Boston society. I am not happy. I
had to leave the house in Ossining but I don't seem to have
arrived at a destination. . . . I've not seen the story since
Esquire sent me neither galleys nor a copy. In a sense it was
your story. It was to you I first read it."

Things went from bad to worse. He narrowly missed
being hit by a car as he crossed Commonwealth Avenue in
a haze. The police threatened to pick him up for public
intoxication — he had lain down on the grass in the Public
Garden to share a bottle of hooch in a paper bag with a
bum who suddenly seemed to be a friend. When he asked if
the policeman knew who he was, the cop made fun of his
accent. They didn't bother to take him in. Anne Sexton
committed suicide. When his old friend Sally Swope invited

him for dinner at her father's house on Beacon Hill, he arrived an hour late, soaking wet (it was raining and he had forgotten an umbrella), and with blood streaming down his face — he had slipped and fallen on the steps to the house.

John Updike was also living alone in Boston that winter. One afternoon when he stopped by Bay State Road to visit, he rang my father's bell and then watched through the glass window of the front door as my father stepped out of his first-floor apartment, letting the door close behind him, and walked down to let him in. He was stark naked, but apparently unaware that there was anything unusual about this. He had just forgotten to put his clothes on. Updike stayed calm, but he anxiously eyed the closed door to my father's apartment. Had it locked automatically? He imagined himself wandering the streets looking for a locksmith — accompanied by the diminutive, distinguished, but totally naked John Cheever. The apartment door was not locked.

By the end of March it became clear to everyone, even the administration of Boston University, that my father was "too sick" to go on teaching. His classes for the rest of the semester were canceled, and his brother Fred rented a car and drove him home to Ossining. When I went out to see him, he didn't seem to know where he was. Day after day he sat in the yellow wing chair in the living room, staring into space. Every now and then he would shake himself out of his daze, but it only took a second for him to remember who he was and how miserable he was and to reach for the big glass at his side. He seemed to be waiting for death, if he was clear enough to be waiting for anything specific. Oblivion was his aim. I think he would have gone anywhere with anyone at that time: a hospital, a rehabilitation center, a permanent sleep, it was all the same to him.

"Boston University was a dreadful mistake," he wrote

Bill Maxwell about ten days after his return. "Anne Sexton killed herself and I never quite got over this. . . . I lived in furnished rooms off Kenmore Square which is a decadent part of town. Every house has a sign in luminous pink that says Apt for Rent. It seemed quite sinister. The walking was wonderful but my memories of the years when I lived in the city were overwhelming and my drinking worsened. So did my heart condition. My dear brother saw that I was in danger and drove me home. I went to the doctor who sent me to the hospital to be dried out. I then went to a psychiatrist who has signed me into a twenty-eight-day clinic for alcoholics. I am allowed out only to go to church on Sundays. This is the Smithers Institute at 56 East 93rd Street. Any mail will be welcome."

Twenty

THE SMITHERS ALCOHOLISM Rehabilitation Unit at 56 East Ninety-third Street in New York City is housed in a gabled beaux-arts mansion that Billy Rose remodeled for himself at the height of his entrepreneurial success. The outside is columned, with wide bay windows, and inside, a marble-lined entryway behind wrought-iron doors faces a grand curved staircase. The ceilings are high, with ornate moldings and paneling, and the bathrooms have mirrored walls intricately engraved with flowery love scenes — garlands and cupids. Behind the house, lower walls outline an elegant formal garden and terrace. The rest of the block as it slopes uphill from Madison to Park Avenue is primarily graceful townhouses and small prewar apartment buildings. Carnegie Hill, as this neighborhood is called, has lately been discovered by real estate developers, and a high-rise condominium, where three bedrooms sell for close to half a million dollars, has just been built across the street.

Smithers is a division of the alcohol rehabilitation program at St. Luke's–Roosevelt Hospital across town; it was established by R. Brinkley Smithers and opened in 1973. The program at Smithers takes twenty-eight days and it is preceded by a week of detoxification in a hospital. During the first two weeks of the program, patients are not allowed out of the building at all — not even into the gardens at the back of the mansion. During the last two weeks they are permitted to leave for an hour on Sunday to go to church. There are two hours of visiting time once a week. Smithers is as much a prison as any prison, and it feels as dangerous. Although there are occasional wealthy or upper-middle-class patients, most of the patients at Smithers in the 1970s were there through Medicaid or on unemployment insurance, and many of them were angry working-class men and women from minority groups. There were fights, unprovoked attacks, and suicides.

"You once wrote that you thought my drinking was suicidal," my father wrote Denny Coates on April 16. "My doctor reached the same conclusion and thus I am here, one of forty-two drug addicts and clinical alcoholics. The scene is a well-preserved, palatial town house. The atmosphere is bizarre. The conditions involve voluntary confinement and it will be twelve days before I can leave these rooms and then only to take holy communion."

Patients at Smithers are assigned household and dining room chores. They eat communally and sleep six or eight to a room on Spartan cots in the grand boudoirs that Billy Rose constructed for himself and his friends. Reading and writing, even letter writing, are firmly discouraged. Instead, patients are encouraged to study *Alcoholics Anonymous*, written by AA founders "Bill W." and "Dr. Bob," and related AA literature. These books and their principles are then applied to each patient's disastrous past life in classes, lectures, and group-therapy sessions. In between there are compulsory exercise classes and films on the same subjects. There is no free time.

Theoretically, anyone at Smithers can walk right out the wrought-iron gates and around the corner to a bar or restaurant and order a drink. Smithers is a voluntary rehabilitation center. But everyone at Smithers knows that the ones who walk out almost always come back again — only the second time they are in even worse shape. The ones inside tell stories about the walkouts who don't come back, too: automobile accidents, fatal heart attacks, "accidental" deaths. By the time they get to Smithers, most people don't have anywhere else to go.

Communication with the outside world is made difficult at Smithers. For the forty to fifty patients, there is one pay telephone mounted on the wall at the busy second-floor landing. The first week my father spent at Smithers, he called me on this telephone every morning to say that he couldn't stand it anymore.

I was working as an editor at *Newsweek* by then, and the calls came into my brightly lit, windowless office down the hall from the noisy hubbub and wire-clacking sounds of the news desk. My father spoke to me in his broken Italian, so that he would not be overheard and understood.

"Non posso, cara," he would say. "Non posso stare qui." He whispered when anyone passed in the hall, and his voice was breaking. I tried to comfort him. I tried to explain why he should stay at Smithers, but really I was terrified. The next call from him, I was sure, would be from some bar around the corner on Madison Avenue — or it would be from the police or from a hospital. I made a reservation for him at Silver Hill, a gentler rehabilitation center in Connecticut, and I parked my car near the *Newsweek* office on Forty-ninth and Madison so that when the call *did* come I would be able to pick him up and get him the care he needed without wasting any time. Every day he sounded worse.

My father shared a room at Smithers with four other men. (There were also two empty beds, one recently vacated by a man who had thrown himself out the window onto the terrace paving two floors below.) His roommates were a ballet dancer, a businessman who had once made a living selling insurance, an unemployed sailor with faded tattoos who smelled like old bilge, and a German delicatessen owner who kept them all awake at night talking to his former customers in his sleep. There are all kinds of people at Smithers, but everyone shares one thing: a desperate addiction to alcohol and drugs. At first it was hard for my father to see what he had in common with a failed male ballerina, a stinking ex-sailor, and a delicatessen owner. No one at Smithers recognized him as a celebrity, or as a successful writer, or even as a cultivated man. That was all bullshit. Instead, they made fun of his accent and mocked his table manners. The intention was clearly to break him; to strip away the specialness and the protective myths he had spent his life perfecting and to reduce him to the irresistible hungers that create an alcoholic. I think we all worried that at the end of this process there would be nothing left of him. We underestimated Smithers, and we certainly underestimated my father.

He didn't break, he changed. Sometime during the middle of April he started to work with the program instead of against it. After the first ten days, his calls to me at *Newsweek* became less frequent, and they lost their panicky edge. Instead, he was funny and relaxed. He told me that as part of his therapy he had to write about everything he had done to hurt each member of his family, and that he wanted to apologize to me for the things he had done. When he had been there three weeks, I went up on Sunday to walk him to church, and he seemed subdued and fragile. A warm light rain was falling, and we stayed under the umbrella I had brought. Instead of going to church we went down Madison Avenue and into Central Park at the Engineers Gate. I could tell that he didn't want to walk too far from Smithers; that was his center now. We talked about writing and André Gide and the way Gide's use of incidental narrative, his stretching of the conventional rules, had excited my father. Then we talked about a friend of his at Smithers who had been a sandhog, and how he had dug his way under the city, under Second Avenue and under the East River and under Central Park. My father was teaching the sandhog how to play backgammon. His sense of humor was back, but he seemed quiet, controlled, and very sad.

"I think I hear some chorale music," he wrote in one of the few journal entries made at Smithers.

One hears almost no music from these back yards. Knowing absolutely nothing about music I conclude, in a scholarly way, that it must be Puccini because of the ascending and melodramatic scale of flats. I once had perfect pitch but that was long ago. Then I hear some dissonance and decide it must be Berg or Schönberg. The soprano then hits a very high note and sustains it for an impossible length of time and I realize that what I've been hearing is the clash of traffic and a police siren amplified by a light rain.

I read Berryman on rehabilitation centers. When I wake this morning my feeling of dislocation is very strong. I am nervous, my vision is poor, I keep singing Dartmouth songs which I can't have heard for years. I'm a sonofagun for beer; I like my whiskey clear/ and if I had a son sir, I'll tell you what he'd do/ he would yell to hell with Harvard like his Daddy used to do.

A heavy rain at five. I am a boy again, a child. I hear the rain strike the air conditioners, watch it gleam on the slate shingles in Thursday's last light. I read, sleep, dream,

wake myself with the loudness of my voice. I am riding,
wearing loafers, and my loafers keep slipping through the
stirrups. Short stirrups said Lila. Did you ride much in Italy.
I never went near a horse in Italy. She still loves you said
the woman with the braids.

After he came out of Smithers and my mother drove him
home to Ossining on May 7, my father never drank again.
He had learned something there, and even more important,
he had formed the basis of a permanent bond with Alcoholics
Anonymous. When he got home, he began attending AA
meetings three to seven nights a week. He took on a sponsor
and eventually sponsored new members. Once every few
weeks he got to meetings early to help with setting up the
chairs and brewing the coffee, and he took turns with everyone else speaking about his experience with alcohol, and the
anxieties that led him to fear that he might drink again.
When he traveled, he felt responsible to his AA group and
his sponsor, and this sense of obligation, of people counting
on him to keep his promises, seemed to help. Often after
dinner he drove to a meeting, and sometimes in the afternoon or morning he would call on his sponsor to talk or go
for a walk or a bike ride with him. Evening after evening, he
sat on folding chairs in basements and parish houses and
listened and tried to help as other members recounted their
battles with booze, the way they hid the empties, the way
they used mints and Sen-Sen and grape-flavored chewing
gum to hide the drink on their breath. In the early 1970s,
before he went to Smithers, my father had gone to a few
AA meetings, but he had found enough excuses not to go
again. They were boring, he complained, or everyone recognized him as a celebrity. Afterward his attitude was different. "I don't go to be entertained," he would say. "I go
because it works." And it did work.

"This place is sometimes cruelly an alkali desert, sometimes Sutter's Mill," he wrote from Smithers to Bill Max-well, who had responded to his plea for mail with long, hand-delivered letters. "The man on my left crochets an-other hat and complains about the administration. He says that if he were strong enough to carry his suitcase down the stairs, he would leave. I've offered to take his suitcase down but he doesn't answer. The ballet dancer is up to his neck in bubble bath, reading a biography of Piaf. I want to get into the toilet, but I can't. It is 8 A.M. The delicatessen owner is sound asleep and asking: 'Haff you been taken care off?' He will be discharged on Monday. He has lost his wife, his children, his house (with the genuine Karastan rug), his delicatessen, his everything. I call Mary from time to time and she is full of complaints. The bank can't add, the dogs (4) are muddy, the lawns are dry. On Sunday morning I shall dress for [church] and ride a bicycle in the park. God knows, God cares, God will understand, God is love and public parks and gardens are his temples."

When my father got home from Smithers he was a differ-ent man. It wasn't just that he didn't drink anymore. The difference in the way he talked and acted was so dramatic that the most astonishing thing for me was the realization of how much he must have changed during the fifteen years his drinking affected him. The changes had been so slow and so painful that I didn't see how complete they were until they were reversed. It was like having my old father back, a man whose humor and tenderness I dimly remembered from my childhood. He was alert and friendly, and for the first time he seemed to join the family instead of just heading it. He was interested in what we were doing and how we felt. And he wanted to learn how to run the washing machine and the dishwasher so that he could help out. It was just nice to be around him in those days. And although he knew too well how easily he could slip, the change in him made it seem less likely than ever that he would. His self-pitying bombast was gone. There were apologies instead of accusations. He was a man who seemed involved with life again — gentle with other people, interested in learning how to help himself, and humorously mocking about his past behavior.

"Day #2," he wrote on his second day back at home and back at work. "I'm still very uptight but I think I won't take Valium. The set piece I'll aim at will be on liberty. There are three points of hazard. One is the euphoria of working at what I think is the best of my ability; one is the euphoria of alcohol when I seem to walk among the stars; one is the euphoria of total sobriety when I seem to command time. That bridge of language, metaphor, anecdote and imagination that I build each morning to cross the incongruities in my life seems very frail indeed."

For all his fears, or perhaps because of them, my father stayed in control. He never took Valium or Librium or Seconal again, although the pills stayed in the medicine cabinet, just as the bottles of gin and whiskey stayed next to the bar in the pantry. In 1978, he also stopped smoking completely after taking a course at Smokenders. In three years he went from being an alcoholic with a drug problem who smoked two packs of Marlboros a day to being a man so abstemious that his principal drugs were the sugar in desserts and his favorite cheap ice cream and the caffeine in the dark, room-temperature "iced" tea that he drank instead of whiskey. But the incongruities in his life remained. His marriage was a battle for scraps of affection, his loneliness was so sharp that it sometimes felt like intestinal flu, and his longing for love from other men increased.

I walk past Ninety-third Street on Madison Avenue once a week on the way to my psychiatrist's office. There are so many psychiatrists on Ninety-sixth Street between Madison and Fifth avenues that it is called the "mental block." Sometimes I cut across Madison and up the hill by Smithers. I pass the imposing columned entry and the wrought-iron gates. I look in at the grand ballroom where my father and I uncomfortably drank acid coffee out of Styrofoam cups one Sunday afternoon during visiting hours. And I think about Smithers and how it changed all of our lives.

"I've been throwing high dice since May and it still goes on," my father wrote Denny Coates, who had been posted to Germany that summer. "I'm not at all worried. I've thrown my share of low dice and I can carry it off. The only difficulty is that all I want to write is a loud shout of love and pleasure. I'm trying to become subtle, melancholy, pallid, urbane and witty — all things I'm famous for and that I, as you well know, have never been."

The future seemed possible again. A little more than a year after he left Smithers, he finished his novel about the prison, which he wrote in a euphoric burst of energy that he seemed to have been storing up during those years of disintegration and collapse. *Falconer* was his most successful novel, and when it was published in 1977 he was on the cover of *Newsweek* and the book was number one on the best-seller lists and sold almost 90,000 copies in hardcover.

In 1978, the year after *Falconer* came out, Knopf published a selection of sixty-one of my father's stories, the first written in 1947 and the last in 1978. He had been reluctant about the collection — it seemed a little too close to living on the past — but Robert Gottlieb had persuaded him to do it and even made the selection of stories from the 119 in the *New Yorker* library and the few others that had appeared in *Esquire*, *Playboy*, and *The Saturday Evening Post*. Gottlieb was right. *The Stories of John Cheever* sold

118,000 copies in hardcover, brought a large paperback advance, and was a main selection of the Book-of-the-Month Club. The book gave him finally the unalterable status of a literary legend — a contemporary hero. The critics drew back in respect. The book won the Pulitzer Prize and the National Book Critics Circle Award.

I had taken a leave of absence from *Newsweek* that year, and my second husband and I were living and writing in a small town near Grasse in France. Even from that distance, I had a sense of the scope of this final, lasting success. And for once my father seemed to be having a wonderful time.

He wrote me in France about a publication dinner for the *Stories* at Lutéce: "The most exciting part of the dinner was when they brought in the first course. This was a fish quish shaped like an enormous pastry fish and decorated with a pastry frigate in full sail. I had Lauren Bacall on my right and Maria Tucci on my left and very much enjoyed myself. Ben [and his wife] were both greatly admired and I was truly proud of them and your mother looked very beautiful. She has a new velvet dress. It is brownish purple and the velvet has been chewed on by French Noblewomen in reduced circumstances. It is very becoming and grand. When I was toasted I told a story and while it wasn't much, Ben observed that everybody sucked air and stared at the ceiling as if they were hearing prophecy. Everyone, that is, but your mother, who kept dropping her table silver. Then everybody stood and held hands and sang: For He's a Jolly Good Fellow. They sang only the first verse. One verse is all they sang. 1."

Twenty-one

My FATHER'S CERTAINTY AS A WRITER was never more apparent than during the year he was writing *Falconer*. When he read from it aloud to us, his voice vibrating with authority and pleasure in his own skill and imagination, it seemed to generate an electricity and excitement that reached outside the circle of listeners slumped in chairs in the library or the living room of the house in Ossining. I think I knew then that the book would be a best seller, and that my parents wouldn't have to worry about money anymore, and that my father was going to be successful and famous in a different way than he had ever been before.

Not only did my father have the energy to write at the top of his talent that year but the timing and the subject were ideal. Each chapter and scene seemed to stream from his imagination already written. These were the things he had been longing to say — the joys and anxieties he had not been able to write about before. *Falconer* is a novel about a man imprisoned for the murder of his brother. He is a heroin addict, and his marriage is a travesty of marriage vows. The center of the book is a tender homosexual love affair. The book's hero, Ezekiel Farragut, is in jail for violating the laws of society. In the end, he is freed from prison and from his addictions by a triumph of love and ingenuity. All these themes were deep in my father's consciousness, and they were to dominate the remaining years of his life.

At the end of May in 1976, as my father was preparing the manuscript of *Falconer* for Knopf's copy editing department, his brother Fred died. Fred was seventy-one, and little more than a year had passed since he had rented a car to drive my ailing father home from his room on Bay State Road in Boston. Fred's daughter Jane had gone to Scituate to visit him and bring him the Sunday paper that morning, and he died quietly in her arms. Fred's death consolidated the uneasy truce my father had reached with his passionate feelings about his older brother. He had wanted to murder Fred — so much that he once told me that it was fear of this fratricidal instinct that forced him to leave home. He had also wanted to live with him. Much of the conflict in my father's heart, and many of the themes in his work, grew out of his love for Fred: the fickle bitchiness of pretty women, for whom Iris Gladwin may have been the first model; the murderous anger of the younger, unwanted brother toward the successful older one; the love of men.

It always struck me that Fred was cheerfully oblivious to the effect he had on my father — and that this made the effect more powerful. Fred was larger and ruddier than my father, athletic where he was runty, public where he was private, loud where he was quiet, bluff and hearty where he was withdrawn and concise. Fred hid his considerable intelligence and erudition behind a hail-fellow-well-met façade that suggested a small-town Rotary dinner.

"Hey, Joey!" he would halloo at my father across a room

— did he notice the almost imperceptible wince? He told a lot of jokes, and they were usually real thigh-slappers. Later, when he had started to drink too much, they were also chandelier-hangers and ass-pinchers and chair-vaulters.

In the 1950s, when Fred and Iris moved to Scarborough, it was obvious that Fred's disintegration was an embarrassment to my father. After a few years they moved up to Westport, Connecticut, and then to Wilton, and after Fred lost his job the family finally scattered, to Colorado and Hawaii and Arizona. Jane married and stayed in Hingham, and Fred came back to Scituate at the end of his life.

Although he looked like my father, Fred had a wide face, a low stance like a boxer's, and a broader accent. He took on the world. I guess you could say that he took on the world and lost — his job, his money, his marriage, his high hopes. But although Fred's rowdiness was pathetic, he maintained a kind of dignity that was enviable — and perhaps infuriating.

"I think I understand it now," my cousin Jane said when I visited her to talk about these two brothers. "My father was the boor." And it's true, Fred was willing to play the boor. His admiration for my father and his talent was unstinting, and his family was raised to admire us, our taste, our culture, our innate classiness, as rigorously as our family was raised *not* to admire Fred and Iris and their way of life. I remember Fred's visits to the house in Ossining to ask for money, and the extreme discomfort in the room; he never stayed for dinner. I remember running into him in Grand Central one hot afternoon and having an electric five-minute conversation about the paintings of John Constable. We didn't dawdle; Fred knew when to leave. By the early 1970s, the two brothers had reached a kind of courteous, conciliatory stand-off — my father was able to accept

Fred's concern about him in Boston — but their feelings for each other were so complicated and so violent that this may have just been a way of avoiding them.

The day after Fred died, my father wrote in his journal, "Cutting the field in the middle of the afternoon in order to plant a cherry tree, I feel how profoundly important such work is to me. Then I recall, by chance, my mother's drinking herself to death and I think of her as uncommonly clear and strong. It is about this time that my brother dies. Alan [Alan Carr, Jane's husband] calls later. I cry. He [Fred] seems as have most people I love, to be lost, to be suffering a loneliness more painful than anything one experiences in life. I read the prayer book but other than that God will not be a stranger the descriptions of life everlasting are not what I have in mind. . . . Susie and I talk about the family. I am inclined to make a legend of the Cheevers and this can easily be done but seems idle to me. I will write a eulogy; including the fact that he wasted half his life."

Later that week, when my father flew up to Boston alone for Fred's funeral at the Norwell Unitarian church, he felt alternately lost and in control. He had never been at home in Boston, but now he noticed the city's ugliness: the huge signs advertising Desenex that ask JOCK ITCH?, the fumes in the Sumner Tunnel, the soapy quality of the local cuisine — lobster rolls, fried clams, baked beans.

"Any tears I shed are facile," he claimed after Fred was buried under a big maple tree at the corner of the Norwell Center cemetery. "The architecture of the early 18th century church is splendid, the smell in the vestibule of heat, wood, and some salt from the sea nearby is I think unique to this part of the world or a lock on my memory. The high arched windows with their many lights must make it a cruel place to worship in the winter but on this splendid summer day they make of the building a frame for the trees and the sky. I do not at all miss my brother. I think that he, with my mother, regarded death as no mystery at all. Life had been mysterious and thrilling I often hear them say but death was of no consequence. Some clinician would say that while I part so easily from my brother I will, for the rest of my life, seek in other men the love he gave me."

My brothers and I had left home by the 1970s; we had each taken up our own lives. Ben was an editor at the *Reader's Digest*, Fred a student at Stanford, I a *Newsweek* editor and a writer. But the last half of the decade was as much a turning point for my father as the mid-fifties had been for the family. Once again, the miserable anxieties of failure and poverty gave way to a glorious success. In June of 1978, he was awarded an honorary degree from Harvard — a triumphant moment for a boy who had dropped out of Thayer Academy. And after the success of *The Stories of John Cheever* that same year, Knopf contracted to pay a $500,000 advance for his next novel. This was not a fortune by famous writers' standards — some authors command advances in the millions — but for my father it was a guarantee of financial security for the foreseeable future, and for the first time in his life he made a few conservative investments.

Travel became increasingly a part of his life. He had the money again, and his situation at home was still difficult. Sometimes it seemed that he went everywhere he was invited — to readings and lectures at universities that a writer of his age and reputation might have been expected to turn down. It was on one of these literary visits, as a three-day teacher and speaker at a western university, that he found what he may have been looking for on all those other trips. He met Rip (as I shall call him, since that was one of my father's names for him in the journals) — the young writer

who would be his close friend, lover, and confidant for the
rest of his life. Rip remembers that when he heard my
father was coming to the university, he decided to avoid him.
Someone else gave my father a story of his, though, and my
father asked to meet him. As a result, Rip's attitude from
the beginning was one of humorous irreverence that was
just my father's style.

"Absolute candor does not suit me, but I will come as
close as possible to describing the chain of events," my
father wrote in his journal in the winter of 1978. "Lonely
and with my loneliness exacerbated by travel, motel rooms,
bad food, public readings and the superficiality of standing
in reception lines I fell in love with Rip in a motel room of
unusual squalor. His air of seriousness and responsibility,
the bridged glasses he wore for his near sightedness and his
composed manner all excited my deepest love."

Rip and my father left the class where they had met, and
after stops at a liquor store — for Rip's whiskey — and at a
supermarket — for my father's ginger ale — they drove to
my father's motel and talked, and they stayed up all night
talking — about their lives, about their women, about writing, and about everything else. When his stint at the university was over, my father went on to Los Angeles, where
he hobnobbed with the stars and wrote long letters to Rip.

My father's advice to the young writer was to get out,
and he did, first going to Yaddo to work, then taking a job
teaching in upstate New York, and finally settling in the
New York suburbs and becoming my father's friend and
literary assistant. Rip and my father continued to talk and
take long walks and bicycle rides together. They had a kind
of joking, mocking sense of humor with each other that
suited my father well. There were anxieties. My father worried about the impact of their relationship on Rip's marriage

— and Rip worried about my parents' marriage, too. He was often at the house in Ossining, and although this was not a comfortable situation for him, he treated my mother with a relaxed courtesy and respect. In fact, he treated her a lot better than my father did. I was always glad to see him. He was pleasant and funny, and when they were together my father seemed more accessible than he usually was. When my mother went up to New Hampshire in the summer, Rip stayed with my father, and for once this annual separation wasn't characterized by angry fights and accusations. Rip even cooked.

Later, when my father was sick, Rip took on the biggest share of the driving, ferrying him back and forth to Memorial Hospital in New York and to Northern Westchester Hospital in Mount Kisco. I was pregnant, and the rest of the family was distracted in other ways; it was Rip who really kept my father company during his last illness.

Although my father allowed himself to enjoy Rip's love more and more in the years after they met, the nature of their friendship was a secret. The idea of homosexuality was still very disturbing to my father, and it was equally disturbing to Rip — a shared concern that made their relationship possible, I think. My father had two sets of fears, a fear that being homosexual might affect him in subtle ways that would end up making him part of the homosexual community he abhorred, and a fear of what the heterosexual community would say if they found out. "And so what I seem to be afraid of is the voice of the world — an estimable place — the voice one thinks of as gossip although it has a true tidal force," he wrote in his journal. "Have you heard? Old Cheever, crowding seventy, has gone Gay. Old Cheever has come out of the closet. Old Cheever has run off to Bessarabia with a hairy youth half his age."

Because of these worries, he and Rip did not run off to Bessarabia or anywhere else together, and they did not rent a house together, and neither of them talked candidly about the other. Rip continued to spend afternoons at the house in Ossining, help my father with his correspondence and literary projects, and sit down at the dinner table as if he was a member of the family. He certainly had more of the family wit and manner than anyone else I could remember, and he seemed to fit in very comfortably, under the circumstances. To protect himself from his fears and his feelings, my father occasionally took on other young "protégés," both literary and sexual, but none was as pleasant or as important. In the four years that I knew Rip, I sometimes had a flicker of wondering about the sexual nature of his friendship with my father, but I dismissed it. I really didn't care. In a way, I think the violent ups and downs of my father's life had exhausted all of us. When my brother Ben told me that they were lovers, I didn't listen, or I put the idea aside. It was only months after my father died, as I was reading his journals, that I found out. I guess what surprised me most was that I hadn't already known. Looking back now, it seems to me that my father's relationship with Rip, for all its painfully obvious problems, was as sweet and satisfying a source of love as love could be for him. His marriage to my mother was not particularly satisfactory, his children were gone, and his mistresses were old or in California. He also saw himself in Rip.

"Dear Rip," he wrote at the beginning of their friendship. "I am truly concerned with your response to what your father said because the greatest and the most bitter mystery in my life was my father. It seemed, from adolescence, that we must learn to love one another. Anything less, it seemed, would wreak some basic damage to my spiritual balance. This problem appears in all the books and stories. It was he who invited an abortionist for dinner. It was he who was discovered drunken, debauched and naked but for a string of champagne corks. He was the drunken old man in the roller coaster when I thought he had drowned himself and he was the old man reading Shakespeare sonnets to the cat. I have finessed these scenes but when he failed me as he did a thousand thousand times, I found my cock and balls in a wringer. I was determined not to lose that sense of locus that I would have lost if I dismissed him as a tragic clown. I persevered, I may have done no more, but it is all part of a chain of being and when you have sons, as you will, it will be easier to comprehend."

Wealth and fame and love had an odd effect on my father. He had spent most of his life in a lonely search for some contribution he might make to literature and civilization, some goal above worldly things, some image of what he called "man's struggle to be illustrious." Now, for the first time, his worldly success was secure and undeniable. He was recognized everywhere and almost universally respected. He was in newspapers and magazines and on television talk shows. The Rockefellers invited him over to their place in Pocantico Hills, and Brooke Astor came for lunch in Ossining. The mail was thick with heavy, engraved invitations and fan letters from other literary lights.

In the heat of all this adulation and security, my father's dignity seemed to thaw. He went through a kind of adolescence of celebrity. At times he seemed to be his own number-one groupie. Conversations with him often reverted to discussions of his own success, his celebrity, and the way Lauren (Betty) Bacall had ardently kissed him the last time they met. He dropped names shamelessly. It was no longer safe to tease him about favorable reviews. In restaurants, he let headwaiters know that he was someone important. Since this kind of behavior was new to him, he wasn't particularly graceful about it. Walking down Park Avenue with him once, after a lunch at the Four Seasons ("Che cosa di buona oggi?"), I noticed that he was smiling his public smile at everyone who passed — just in case they recognized him, I suppose. I once drove out to Ossining and found him intently listening to his new Walkman; it was a tape of him reading one of his old stories, "The Death of Justina." And in many ways he seemed to be listening, most of the time, to his own voice.

Twenty-two

Aт тне beginning of June, 1982, I drove out to Ossining to visit. I had gone out often that spring, driving up the West Side Highway and the Saw Mill River Parkway to Route 9A, or over the Willis Avenue Bridge and onto the Major Deegan Expressway. Sometimes my husband and the baby, Sarah, came with me, especially when my father was well enough to enjoy seeing her. This time I knew he wasn't. It was one of the summer's first brutal days, and as I drove up through Ardsley and Dobbs Ferry, the back of my shirt stuck to the vinyl of the driver's seat and hot, dusty air blew in across my neck from the parched grass shoulders of the road. The irises and delphiniums were out in my mother's garden, and the lawns looked dry.

In the upstairs bedroom where my father lay, the air was heavy and stifling. A small heater I had bought blasted away on its highest setting next to the bed. My father was cold. He was always cold. In the autumn, before we knew how sick he was, he complained of chills and shivering. We had urged him to go south for the winter. At Christmas he lay under piles of blankets and quilts. In January and Feb-

ruary no clothes or covers could warm him. But when the
weather turned balmy and then hot, he still wore sweaters
and stayed in bed.

On the day of this visit, I stood at the end of the bed
sweating. "Does he want the heater turned off?" I asked my
mother.

It was hard for my father to speak. He looked over at the
heater and then up at me. "Unplugged," he mumbled in his
weakened voice — or something that sounded like "unplugged." My father never trusted electrical appliances. If
a heater, toaster, or electric blanket was turned off without
being unplugged, he was convinced it might still flash on
mysteriously, with fiery and explosive consequences.

"I think he just wants it turned off," my mother said, and
then, in a louder voice, "John! Don't you just want it turned
off?"

"Maybe he wants it unplugged too," I said. He often did;
on the other hand, if he only wanted it turned off for a few
minutes he probably did not want it unplugged. My mother
reached down and turned off the heater. I stepped behind it
and yanked the plug out of the wall.

My father lifted his head and we both turned to look at
him. From his face, I knew that I had done the wrong thing.
"How clever of you, Susie," he spoke in a high cracked
voice. Each word took a long time. "How *clever* of you to
think I wanted it unplugged." His words were slurred and
faint, but his sarcasm was unmistakable. My mother looked
down at the blankets. It brought back all those other times.
How clever of you, Susie, to have brought me aspirin when
I'm supposed to be taking Tylenol! How clever of you to
arrive at precisely the wrong moment and to say precisely
the wrong thing! How clever of you to do things so completely incorrectly that it almost seems clever.

As I stood there at the end of the bed, my heart just sank.

I had come out from the city to love him; I couldn't do it. I reminded myself of all the love and reassurance that had passed between us during his illness. I remembered his delight in the baby. I told myself that he was dying, he was in pain, he didn't mean it, he wasn't responsible. Nothing helped. He didn't love *me*, obviously; how could I love him?

I was always afraid of my father. Requests to him were sometimes quickly granted but other times deflected by his sarcasm or his agility with words — their real meaning obscured. To ask him for money was to risk a humiliating verbal sally, especially if he intended to give it to you.

I remember that in 1977, the year *Falconer* was published, I decided to ask him for a $5000 loan. *Newsweek* was becoming more and more difficult for me as I realized that I wanted to try and write a novel. I resolved to take a loan from him to finance some time off. Twice I drove out to Ossining for the purpose of asking him, but somehow I just couldn't do it. Maybe I didn't have the nerve. Maybe I wasn't ready to write a novel yet. "He would have annihilated you," my brother Ben says now when I ask him what I was so afraid of. In our family, no one ever asked for help. Weakness was treated as a temporary aberration, and failure was a bad joke. It took another year, and the encouragement of my second husband, Calvin Tomkins, before I was ready to collect my savings and back vacation pay, sell my car, sublet my apartment, and go off to write my first novel. I didn't ask my father for money. He agreed to baby-sit my dog, Sheba, while we were away.

During the time my father was publishing *The Stories of John Cheever* and *Oh What a Paradise It Seems*, I wrote and published three novels. My father and I were close enough to establish a complicated and tacit agreement about this unusual situation. We decided not to deal with it. I never showed my father anything I had written until it had been bought by a publishing house and was in final manuscript form. I didn't ask for help, and he didn't offer it. When he did read my novels, he was polite but perfunctory. "I liked it very much," he would say, or "I thought it was fine."

In other ways he was more enthusiastic about my writing. He developed a running literary scorecard: Dumas (2), Bellow (1), Theroux (2), Updike (3) — both John Updike's mother and son are published fiction writers — and exulted in our new parity. When my books were successful in terms of book-club or movie sales, he was pleased and congratulatory. When I ran into trouble with editors, he told me about his troubles with editors and advised me to trust myself. When I was devastated by bad reviews, he told me about the attacks he had survived and suggested that writing about my feelings might help me as it had helped him. In public, he praised me and, if necessary, my work. In private, we never talked about the writing part of writing; instead we discussed agents and editors and subsidiary rights and publishing practices, or we joked about what it must have been like at the Dumas dinner table or whether Updike had any cousins in the wings who might upset our score. The important thing about this was that it worked very well. There was very little tension between us about the fact that we were both writing fiction, and in the last years of my father's life we got along better than we had for some time. During the year I spent abroad writing my first novel, we wrote each other long letters two or three times a week. This is what he wrote in October of 1978, when he heard I had finished my first book:

Dear Susie,

Our affectionate and enthusiastic congratulations on having completed your novel. We are all very proud of you. Scything, I think, is the best thing to do when you complete a work of fiction but I don't suppose you could do that in

[France] without causing some talk. I seed lawns, hang storm windows and fell trees. I also pray — no less — for contrition and humility and when I achieve these — always in excess — I go back to scything. I think that to complete a novel is a great accomplishment.

There is no truth at all in the gossip about Bathsheba and me — but don't tell the book reviewers. Entre nous, we aren't getting along. She accompanied me yesterday into the pine woods to cut down some trees. The noise of the axe deeply offends her but she curls up cutely on the pine needles, directly in the fall line and does her worst imitation of Mary Pickford, selling matches in a blizzard. This is dreadful. Then when the tree is about to fall and I pull her out of danger she runs screaming down to the house with tales of rape, mayhem and plunder. The only bonds we have are illusory. She thinks the [neighbor's] cat still lives. I think *The New York Times* is still published [the *Times* was on strike when this letter was written]. At dawn we climb the hill together — she for the cat, me for the paper. When we both return to the house empty-handed there is a fleeting moment of shared disappointment. For the rest of the day our relationship is oaths, whimpering, imprecations, sidelong glances and slammed doors.

His journal entry for the day is brief and equally enigmatic. He describes a gala party at the Rockefeller estate in Pocantico Hills and then a dinner dance at the Sleepy Hollow Country Club in Scarborough. Nature is extolled. He concludes, "And this morning I recall how, as a young man, I chose to go out with the wood crew and fell trees. This is still my choice and I pray that it is not perverse. That it is not my choice to see such a view through the dirty window of a whore's room where I have exhausted my nature of what is forbidden and will presently have the shit beaten out of me. Ben ran the marathon in 2:59, in the 800 group among 11,000 contestants. Susie has completed a novel. None of us, particularly me, are first rate but we do, I like to think, persevere."

While I was still abroad he wrote, "Bathsheba is quite ready for the book jacket as well as for the photograph for the review and the advertisements. So are Edgar and Mazie. They feel that loving dogs and a view of a stone wall will help sell books; and I think they're right, but someone is bound to point out that Simon & Schuster and Knopf are using the same dogs. Who owns the dogs? Gulf and Western? RCA? It would make a great piece for *The New Republic*. WNET is rerunning the Cavett interview where I thank you for having made it so easy for your parents to love you. This brings up my gratefulness to you for the tact you've displayed in embarking on a literary career. Your independence has been peerless."

Family harmony was the center of my father's sense of personal security. He often said that he couldn't bear to leave the land he had tilled and cleared, the house he had paid for, the familiar interiors, the dogs he loved so well. He avoided argument with me and my brothers, especially as we got older and were home less of the time. He did not divorce my mother. He wanted us all together under one roof, joking and smiling and having fun, and he was willing to suppress a great deal to achieve this. It was worth it. The house in Ossining always seemed like an important place to be, and I think we each drew tremendous comfort from the close circle of family that he assembled there.

"It is after dark; just. A summer night, stars and fire flies. The last night in June," he wrote one evening in Ossining when my brother Ben was home from school. "My oldest son stands on the bridge over the brook with a Roman candle. He is a man now. His voice is deep. He is barefoot and wears chinos. It takes two or three matches to light the fuse. There is a splutter of pink fire, a loud hissing, the colored fire is reflected in the water of the brook and lights the voluminous clouds of smoke that roll off the candle. The light changes from pink to green, from green to red. It makes on the trees and in the heavy air an amphitheatre or sphere of unearthly light. In this I see his beloved face, his figure. I cannot say truthfully that I have never felt anything but love for him. We have quarrelled . . . But all of this is gone. Now there is nothing between us but love and good natured admiration. The candle ends with a loud coughing noise and voids a spate of golden stars and a smell of brimstone. He drops the embers into the brook. Then the dark takes over but I think that I have seen something splendid. This young man, the weird and harmless play of colored light, the dark water of the brook."

We had wonderful times. A simpler way to put this is that my father loved his children. The three of us were, as he said, "the roof and settle" of his existence. As individuals we often displeased him, but as a unit we were cherished and indispensable.

Twenty-three

IN THE LAST YEARS OF HIS LIFE, my father had achieved both wealth and fame. He had won all the prizes and his books had been translated into a dozen languages and hit the top of the best-seller list. His stories had been adapted for the stage and the movie and television screen, and in the summer of 1981 Channel 13 filmed *The Shady Hill Kidnapping* (aired in 1982), a drama for which he had written the screenplay — something he had been wanting to try for years. But his life at the house in Ossining didn't reflect this celebrity; his daily schedule was routine and rather ordinary. Being outside the city isolated him from the effects of success, and the afternoon mail was often the high point of the day. He thought of moving into New York, and even looked at a few apartments, but it was too hard for him to imagine living alone in two rooms without the house or the lawns. I remember that he asked me how I would feel if my father was an old man walking through Greenwich Village with a dog on a rope, and I laughed. He didn't leave. Instead, he stayed in the Ossining house, living out the pleasant uneventful days of a somewhat unorthodox suburban squire.

He always woke up early. When I spent the night there, I could hear him thump down the stairs at six or seven, followed by the whirl and scrabble of hungry dogs and cats on their way after him. He hated the cats, but he fed them. Then he shaved and made coffee so strong that no one else could drink it, and Edgar would join him for a walk up the driveway to get the *New York Times* from the newspaper tube. After breakfast he retired upstairs to my brother Ben's old room at the top of the house. He worked at Ben's student desk next to sagging shelves of schoolbooks and Ben's single bed — often occupied by Edgar. The only real signs of his occupancy were the portable typewriter and a stack of papers and mail, a few Alcoholics Anonymous books, and a full-page ad from *Cosmopolitan* showing a scantily clad woman reading a hardcover copy of *The Stories of John Cheever* in bed. His working schedule was as flexible when he was a famous man writing *Oh What a Paradise It Seems* as it had been when I was a child. If the telephone rang, he answered it, he wrote letters to everyone who wrote him, and he often took a break to drive the maid home or do some shopping.

An occasional guest or journalist or student would come for lunch, which was eaten downstairs in the dining room. My mother served soup, a salad, and cheese and crackers or bread, and my father usually peeled himself a piece of fruit for dessert. He considered the ability to peel fruit without touching it to be a mark of European sophistication. On Fridays, he and two or three old friends from the neighborhood who were retired or worked at home would go out to Ronnie's, a local Italian restaurant, for lunch. All the waitresses knew them — they called themselves The Friday Club. Sometimes Don Ettlinger or Edward Newhouse drove across the river to have lunch, but they were the only writers in this group. The others were usually Arthur Spear, Barrett Clark, Tom Glazer, the songwriter and singer, and Roger Willson, who lives in Briarcliff Manor. After lunch Arthur and Roger would often go back to my father's house for a game or two of backgammon.

In the evenings, after AA meetings, my father often dropped in on his friends Eugene and Clare Thaw, who lived in a big Stanford White house in Scarborough, across from Beechwood. On Sunday mornings he drove into Ossining to a store named Say Cheese, where he bought croissants that he took to Sara Spencer's house, across Cedar Lane from his own driveway, for breakfast. Arthur Spear and Sara Spencer, the Thaws and the Willsons, his own family and Rip, these were the people my father saw most of the time. Other neighbors — the Reimans, the Zieglers, the Benjamins, the Rickses, and Marion Ascoli — dropped by sometimes, or my parents went to their houses for dinner. His neighbors were much more a part of his life than the occasional celebrities he met and entertained.

After dinner on a slow summer evening, he would drive the dogs to the Carvel stand in Croton and buy them all chocolate flying saucers — Edgar's favorite. In the afternoons he liked to go to the local mall, the Arcadian Shopping Center, or to the discount supermarket where the Grand Union had been in Croton. He would cruise up and down the aisles buying ice cream or a head of lettuce and eavesdropping on conversations at the checkout counter. He liked to guess about people's characters and destinations from the contents of their shopping carts.

My father did all his shopping in Ossining. Even serious jewelry he gave as presents often came from the local jewelry store in the Arcadian Shopping Center, which generally featured hearts on chains and bracelets spelling out names like Kimberley and Tracy. Everyone in town seemed to know my father, and everyone hailed him as a friend and local figure. He was the kind of man who inspired loyalty and good will in shopkeepers and garage men — he always gave incredible tips — and dropping his name was usually a good way to get the tires changed faster or the groceries delivered on time. When he walked down Main Street, men and women stopped to chat or shake his hand, people he knew from the prison or the volunteer fire department or AA or some other civic group. We used to call him the Mayor of Ossining.

But in spite of the small-town roots he had so carefully cultivated, my father suffered from severe disorientation as he approached his seventieth year. Sometimes he literally didn't know where he was. The run-down familiarity of the town, the comforting eighteenth-century lines of his house, the acres of land he had mowed and cleared, the neat lines of his vegetable garden — these were his mileposts. He hated to go into New York City. Grand Central Terminal terrified him, and the speeding packs of cars on F.D.R. Drive seemed dangerous and out of control. The hundreds of strange faces and the dozens of new skyscrapers were too much change. When he did go into the city, for a party he felt he had to attend, or a literary event, or to have dinner with us, he appeared supremely charming and in control. He wasn't. His laugh was nervous and his body tense. This anxiety made it even harder for him not to drink.

Although he lacked natural athletic talent, my father loved physical exercise and depended on it. "Oh ho ho!" he would shout with pleasure as he plunged into a swimming pool or down a ski slope or pushed off into a skating pond. During his last years, his daily workout became the focus of each afternoon. In the summer he went for long bicycle rides on his new ten-speed, with Rip or anyone else who was available. He would pedal up over the hill at Cedar Lane and down to Glendale Road, past Marion Ascoli's house, where he often stopped to talk with her farm manager and pick up a dozen fresh eggs, past Teatown Lake and the Swopes' old stables, which were the scene of the New Year's Eve revels he and my mother had gone to so long ago, and home on Quaker Ridge, past the Malsins' and the house where the Boyers used to live before they moved away. Sometimes a friend along the route would hail him and he would stop and talk for a minute. Afterward he often went up to Sara Spencer's house for a swim in her pool.

Summers were also the time for fertilizing the lawns and spading and planting his vegetable garden. Although my father hired people to mow the lawns and chop the wood when he couldn't do these things anymore, he still spent a great deal of time on his property. My brother Fred wrote, "I also want to say that he undoubtedly felt that redemption could be achieved through simple physical work carried on out of doors, and it stands to his credit that in his later years, no matter what his preoccupations, he spent more time weeding the garden (while discussing Carlos Fuentes with Edgar) and brush hooking the orchard than he did having sexual affairs with men or women or basking in the glow of his literary success."

In the winter, my father's afternoons were spent skating. Tremendous time and energy went into worrying about the quality of the ice on the various local ponds. If it had snowed, the ice would need shoveling. A sudden thaw could ruin everything. The best ice, very rare and usually found only at Teatown Lake, was the black ice produced when the water froze very quickly. Through this translucent surface a skater could see the bottom of the lake and the underwater plants waving gently in the currents under the ice. He skated on Teatown Lake and he skated at Sara Spencer's pond and he skated at the old Kress estate, which had been taken over by a charitable organization for wounded veterans called the 52 Association. The Association's land adjoined ours, and over the years there had been a series of encounters about our family's right — claimed by us — to walk our dogs across their property to the land on the other side and to use their pond occasionally for swimming and skating. In the late 1970s, the 52 Association started a series of improvements on their land that brought an end to these encounters and our trespassing. They filled in a small swamp and dug up the meadow at our edge of the property. The old path across the fields was rendered impassable. The broad meadow, which had once been the estate's archery field, became a morass. *Oh What a Paradise It Seems* is a novel about an old man who loves to skate. He tries to save the pond he skates on from becoming a dumping site, and it is saved in spite of him. The novel has a sad elegiac quality, as if he were writing about some other time, some other man, some other world.

In more temperate weather, my father loved to take long walks — his favorite was the path along the Croton Aqueduct, through woods and back yards, over the lawns of the General Electric plant, and high above the Croton River, to where it opened onto the grassy ravine in front of the Croton Dam. In the spring, the dam overflowed and water cascaded down its huge, stepped spillway with a roar that could be heard for a mile.

My mother is a wonderful cook. My parents ate dinner early, and after my father tucked in his chicken with rice and broccoli or his pot roast and vegetables, he often drove to an AA meeting. He went to meetings at four local chapters: the Croton meeting in the parish house of the church just down the street from Ronnie's Italian restaurant; the Briarcliff meeting in the parish house of the Congregational church; the Chappaqua meeting; and the Scarborough meeting in the parish house of the Presbyterian church just across Route 9 from Beechwood and the little house where we once lived. My father became a well-known figure at these meetings, not just because he went to a lot of them or because he was a celebrity but because of his incisive manner, his self-mocking humility, and his desire to help other people as he had been helped and as he was being helped. He used the weight of his success to make himself a convincing example. But when my father discussed his own problems and anxieties at meetings, he stayed away from the specific issues. Even there, he maintained a certain reserve, talking about his struggles in vague, metaphorical language. My father didn't like to talk about his own needs. AA holds meetings for writers and homosexuals and almost every other kind of special group, but my father wasn't interested. Although he kept his distance, "the program" was still in many ways the center of his life. It was because of it that he had a life at all, and he didn't forget this.

As he got older, my father said that one of his problems was that he still thought of himself as a teen-ager. He had the passions and enthusiasms of youth long after they were appropriate. This kept him looking and behaving years younger than he was, but it also made the limitations of old age almost impossible for him to accept. It took three heart attacks and a dozen hospitalizations to teach him that he couldn't just dive into a cold swimming pool, or tear down the dunes into the surf, or stay up all night reading and drinking. Moderation was not natural to him. With age, and with the absence of the oblivion that alcohol had provided for him, he found himself feeling increasingly out of place even at home.

"Old age seems to have presented me with two discernible changes. I think these constitutional," he wrote in 1980. "One is an increase in fear. In reading of a Vermont winter I think not of skiing in the mountains in the morning light: I think only of the cold as some premonition of death. I think only of pain. And watching on TV a film of some waves breaking on a shore in the early morning I think how far I have gone from this light, this freshness, this sense of being a happy participant."

In the late 1970s, he also had begun to suffer from attacks of what he called otherness. He would be breaking an egg for breakfast and suddenly feel he was in a hotel room in Kiev, or standing in his mother's kitchen in Wollaston. A smell or a sound could transport him out of time into a terrifying, unknown, other dimension. His brain missed a beat and he could not remember his name or where he was. "I do not know who I am or where I am," he wrote after one such lapse. "This is easily corrected with movement — I efficiently plant a row of broccoli, but I think it should be observed should it worsen. I mentioned it to the doctor and got no response. It is the sense of a level of consciousness that I do not comprehend — some firmament beyond the mind very much like the structures in space — this is the imagery — but, for a moment, overwhelming. I am not in this world."

These lapses were as unexpected as they were unprecedented. My father could be bicycling along Cedar Lane with Rip, or chatting with Sara Spencer by her swimming pool, when his mind seemed to slip out of the present and into a timeless emptiness. The specific images that often triggered this state were related to my father's past, his alcoholism, women he had known, his own clumsy innocence. The reverie would often begin with the images of J., the promising young writer who had become a drunk, and G., a chic, cynical beauty who had been married to one of my father's oldest friends. In the daydream, G. was walking down the beach at Wauwinet on Nantucket and saying something cutting over her shoulder about my father's lack of under- standing — his phony boyishness. J. was standing in a dingy bar somewhere singing a forlorn song about not having something that he needed. The "Ain't Got Nothing" song, my father called it. These pictures would flash into my father's mind without warning, and when they did he lost all other sense of place and time. The tune J. was singing in the reverie was a song my father knew well, but it eluded his conscious memory. If he could remember the song, he told me, he thought he might go mad.

"I have spiritual and emotional vertigo several times dur- ing the week," he wrote in 1980 after his return from a trip to Rumania. "I seem to be confronted with some cynical social contract and an underprivileged male who sings a song about his forlornness. Throw in a pretty face and a seascape and I seem to be falling into madness. . . . Twice since my return I have endured the sense of otherness. I am about to say to my daughter, sitting yesterday by an open fire, that I have returned home only to have refreshed the sense that there is no home, there is no surety or permanence in this world. I shut up."

Sometimes he felt that this sense of otherness was the price he was paying for having pushed his imagination to its outer limits. At other times he was afraid that years of hard drinking, chain-smoking, and drugs had damaged his brain. Small lapses of memory upset him. And in the fall of 1980, his fears that something had gone awry were dra- matically confirmed. He was staying at Yaddo to work on *Paradise* when it happened. After an afternoon of bicycling, he ate dinner and watched the World Series on television with a group of other writers and artists. In the bottom half of the seventh he went into convulsions and collapsed on the floor in a coma.

He described the incident in his journal eight days later:

This is Tuesday morning a week after the last entry. I cashed a check and bicycled around Saratoga Lake, a distance of 22 miles. On the bicycle trip I passed cottages called Gud Enuff and Dun Roamin, I tried to strike some mature perspective on the pleasure to be found in such cottages on a hot summer's day. I regard them with contempt although I know nothing about them. The road takes me onto the old Route 9 — yesterday's strip — the encampments of yesterday's nomads and transients of a decade ago. The lures are still out for strays who took the wrong turn or latecomers who found all the beds taken in more desirable neighborhoods. The shingles on one club read: Bar, Dancing, Casino, Go-go Girls, Hawaiian cooking, Horses for Rent, Open, For Sale. Fatigue is something I sought and seem to have enjoyed on my return. I spoke with George . . . and wrote a letter to Mary in my studio. I ate dinner with the company and went to an AA meeting. This is one of the gatherings where the sense of an encounter is forceful. I returned to my studio and watched the ball game with Maryann, Joan and Lee. In the seventh inning I suffer a convulsion called a grand mal seizure. I completely lose consciousness and come to in the emergency room of the Saratoga Hospital. . . . In the morning, my determination to avoid hazardous investigations of my brain finds me in an ambulance, speeding south. I move into the hospital at home and am given tests for two days. Nothing is concluded; nothing is discovered. M. is loving and patient, and I cannot really recall a time when she has so unselfishly given herself to me.

My father's first seizure, and the second, which occurred a few months later during a backgammon game at the Willsons' house, seemed to begin the end of his life. Although there is apparently no medical evidence to connect his seizures with the cancer that killed him, it was just a little more than a year after the first seizure that the cancer was diagnosed. The seizures changed other things, too. Now the fear of death, of some mysterious darkness and cold, had more than a symbolic significance. Dilantin, the drug he took twice a day to prevent another seizure, was a depressant. His marriage, on the other hand, took a dramatic turn for the better. Suddenly my parents were friends again. My mother proudly told stories about my father's sweetness to her — he had driven to an antique fair in Chappaqua to buy her an Imari dish that she had mentioned as being beautiful but too expensive, and he hired an architect to begin drawing up plans for a private studio for her on the east side of the house.

But his painful, threatening sense of otherness and loss was intensified. When he went back to work on *Paradise*, the words seemed unfamiliar and shallow, as if they had been written by someone else. He had to start over, and he told his friend Clare Thaw that he was hurrying the book because he was afraid he didn't have much time.

His anxiety about his loving friendship with Rip increased. He wondered if the seizures were some kind of punishment for his enjoyment of another man's love. He encouraged Rip to leave him, but he was afraid that Rip would leave him. Illness also made it much harder not to drink. Why shouldn't he have a drink, if he was going to be sick anyway? He spent more and more time talking with his AA sponsor.

"When it grows dark I would like a drink," he wrote. "The Hemingway stories — or stories about nada — the utter nothingness that is revealed to an old man — seem to correspond to what I've experienced in these last few months. I do believe in God's will and the ordination of events, and perhaps it is stupid of me to question the ordination of my lying on the floor convulsed and senseless. It did bring my wife back to me and I have never asked for anything more. I feel perhaps that the sorrow of these days will be revealed as having had their usefulness. What is the nature of this sorrow is bewildering. I seek some familiarity that eludes me. I want to go home and I have no home."

In the spring of 1981, my father finished his last novel, *Oh What a Paradise It Seems*, and turned it in. The editors at Knopf had hoped for a "big" novel, a blockbuster to consolidate the reputation he had gained through the success of the *Stories*. My father had wanted to write a big novel. But instead he wrote a 100-page, sadly triumphant story about an old man who tries to save the pond he loves to skate on. The tale is haunting and wonderful, "a story to be read in bed in an old house on a rainy night."

In June of 1981, my father was admitted to Phelps Memorial Hospital for a recurrent urinary problem, and the doctors operated to remove his right kidney. For a while after this operation, he seemed to get better every day. His life seemed again to be both precious and navigable.

"So I sit at the kitchen table drinking black coffee and thinking of Verdi," he wrote after breakfast one morning that summer. "I think of the enormous contribution Verdi made to the life of the planet and the enormous cooperation he was given by orchestras and singers and the enthusiasm of orchestras. And I think of what an enormous opportunity it is to be alive on this planet. Having myself been cold and hungry and terribly alone I think I still feel the excitement of that opportunity. The sense of being with some sleeping person — one's child or one's lover — and seeming to taste the privilege of living, of being alive."

Oh What a Paradise It Seems was published in March 1982 and respectfully reviewed, along with a novel by the Indian writer R. K. Narayan, on the front page of the *New York Times Book Review*. In the fall of 1981, my father worked hard at the round of prepublication interviews that accompanies the promotion of a book. He came into New York for reporters and received them in Ossining, presenting, as usual, the façade of a charming, urbane literary gentleman. The effort seemed to tire him, and his impatience was sometimes quite evident.

"I find myself greatly fatigued," he wrote, at home after a marathon day of interviews and photo sessions in New York. "I am pleased to make coffee in the kitchen and chat with the old dog. I am Bette Davis and the old dog is Geraldine Fitzgerald in the last scenes of *Dark Victory*. 'Now we have to learn to live again,' says the old dog. And I say 'If I can laugh I can live.' "

But by November he began to lose the health he had seemed to regain after his kidney operation in the spring. He weakened almost imperceptibly. For once he seemed to mellow and enjoy his accomplishments, and he also seemed to get back the self-mocking humor that had been lost when he became a celebrity. At the same time, he began to lose weight, and his eyes looked oddly larger in his thin face.

"Thanksgiving Day," he wrote, two weeks before his disease was diagnosed as terminal. "Thanksgiving Day and the presence of our daughter so pleases me that Thanksgiving and gratefulness do not, for me, cover the feeling of requition that I enjoy in watching her straighten her husband's hair. Her brothers call and their news contributes to my sense of requition. Mary swears at the turkey but would one want a wife who sang as she basted the bird? The day is all very pleasant, the meal excellent and I go to AA."

Twenty-four

W<small>HEN WE LIVED IN</small> Rome, my father used to take
me to outdoor concerts at the Basilica of Constantine. It was
a romantic time for us — I was just thirteen that summer
— and the most romantic of settings. The drums and brasses
echoed and boomed around the ornate stone entablature of
the basilica's three archways, and behind us the columns
and ruined temples of the Roman Forum gleamed in the
dark. One evening the orchestra played Rimsky-Korsakov's
Scheherezade, the musical version of the *Arabian Nights*.
My father thought this music was unbelievably corny, and
for each musical phrase he produced *sotto voce* a scene
in a mock-melodramatic narrative: (*Violins and flutes*) "A
woman is sitting at a table reading by candlelight . . .
(*horns and drums*) a man's face appears at the window . . .
(*solo clarinet*) a fair-haired child runs into the room . . ." and
so forth.

As I think back on the last six months of my father's
life, the months just before and after December 6, which
was the Saturday the doctors said that he was dying, each

day seems to be scored with those same melodramatic orchestral instruments. In the early fall we take a long bicycle ride, the last one, up over Cedar Lane and down Glendale. Autumn leaves are falling, the air is cold (*woodwinds, violins, flutes*). At Thanksgiving my father seems frail but very happy (*violins, a sonorous, foreboding clarinet*). By Christmas he is weaker and we bring him the gifts as he lies in bed (*drums, bassoons, the low drone of the bass*). Sickness, cancer, death — these things are hard to describe because of what we expect. But in spite of the enormity of what was happening to our family as my father died, we all went on day after day, making telephone calls and eating cereal for breakfast, getting dressed in the morning and going off to work, visiting the hospital and getting our own physical checkups, shopping, worrying about eating too much or drinking too much or not having enough money. There is no sudden suspension of everyday life when terrible things happen. Death is terrifying because it is so ordinary. It happens all the time.

First my father had a series of radiation and chemotherapy treatments at Memorial Hospital in New York, and then he had more chemotherapy treatment at Northern Westchester Hospital in Mount Kisco. Sometimes the doctors were discouraged — they changed the chemotherapy treatments twice, and it was clear that this was because the treatments weren't working — but usually they were optimistic. There would be weeks when my father seemed a little better, but he slowly and steadily got worse. On April 12 I had my baby, Sarah Liley Cheever Tomkins, at New York Hospital, and Rip drove my parents in to see me the next day. My father looked nervous and breakable. During the early treatments, he had set great store by the fact that he hadn't gone bald from chemotherapy as many patients did, but by April most of his hair was gone. At the end of April he was awarded the National Medal for Literature; he was able to accept the honor in a ceremony at Carnegie Hall and to give a short speech.

"What I am going to write is the last of what I have to say," he wrote in the journal, composing this speech. "I will say that literature is the only consciousness we possess and that its role as consciousness must inform us of our ability to comprehend the hideous danger of nuclear power. Literature has been the salvation of the damned, literature has inspired and guided lovers, routed despair and can perhaps in this case save the world."

My father died late in the afternoon of June 18. The light was already fading, but the heat remained in that dark upper bedroom. Three days before, he had fallen while trying to get out of bed and walk, and his leg had broken. After that, we had taken turns injecting him with morphine, and a nurse had come to help. The afternoon he died was a Friday, and she had already gone home for the day. My brother Ben was there, and my mother and Calvin and the baby.

About five-thirty, the minister came from Trinity Church to say the last rites. He put on his white robe and lit the candle and opened the ointment. The heat made sweat marks around the edges of his curly hair. "Bless O Lord thy servant, John," the minister intoned. It was dark and he had trouble reading the prayer book as he recited the service. Under the bedcovers my father kicked his legs and flailed an arm. Was he welcoming the minister, or trying to banish him? The voice droned on. Finally the minister made the sign of the cross on my father's forehead.

"Our Father who art in heaven, hallowed be thy name," we prayed together, standing there at the end of the bed next to my mother's Chippendale desk, my husband holding the baby behind us. I watched my father's face, refined to skeletal features as he tossed on the pillow. It's just a precaution, I said to him silently. This doesn't mean you have to die. It was harder and harder for him to breathe. Afterward the minister stood over him for a moment and we all said "Amen," then I stepped back to be next to my husband and hold the baby. I heard a little coughing noise, and when I turned around, my father was dead.

It was so fast; it was so fast! One moment he was still my father, the next moment he was a dead man. We all kissed him and I drew the sheet up over his shoulders. We went to and fro in the room where he lay, making telephone calls, getting things. The minister held the baby. My husband called the police. Ben called the doctor. I called the funeral home. Ben called my brother Fred in California. My mother opened the closet to get the clothes for the undertaker, the clothes my father would be buried in. She took out his gray suit with the rosette from the American Academy of Arts and Letters in the buttonhole, and the pair of loafers he had bought with me one day at a store near the Plaza Hotel. We chose a blue shirt and a pink and gray tie that a friend had made for him. When I saw the clothes draped over a chair next to where my father lay, I started to cry.

A young policeman came, and then a detective, and then the man from the funeral home. They opened a folding stretcher with torn green covering, and we watched as they rolled my father's body off the bed and onto the canvas. They had trouble getting the stretcher around the turn in the stairs — it's an old house — and they lifted it over the banister. Then we all walked down the stone steps past the yew trees and the rhododendron to the driveway, and they loaded the stretcher into the back of a black station wagon and the man from the funeral home drove it up the hill. "Don't cry," my mother said. "He isn't really dead; he lives on in us."

* * *

On Monday we drove up to Norwell. There was a simple service in the church, and there were a lot of people I hadn't seen in a long time and a lot of photographers. John Updike read his eulogy, and my brothers each talked about their memories of my father, and I read the lesson from the New Testament. Then we walked across the green to the cemetery and watched as they lowered my father into the grave next to his brother Fred and next to his mother and father. The grave was deep and steepsided, and you could see that the sides cut neatly through some roots from the big maple tree overhead. Our heels sank into the grass of the churchyard, and I remembered how my father loved the sound of a woman's high heels, the rustle of a dress, the sweetness of perfume. I remembered waiting downstairs with him while my mother dressed for a party, and the way the sound of her high heels above us meant that she was almost ready. They took the American flag off the coffin and folded it and handed it to my mother, and then they lowered the coffin into the grave. The minister said some prayers and the words about ashes to ashes, dust to dust. We walked away from the grave and out through the gates of the cemetery to the cars. On Wednesday there was a memorial service in Ossining at Trinity Church, and Saul Bellow gave a eulogy and Bud Benjamin and Gene Thaw talked about the ways they remembered my father and we sang some hymns and the minister said a lot of prayers.

* * *

The following year, when I go back to my father's grave, there are high drifts around the churchyard, and I clamber over them and stand knee deep in the snow where his headstone will be. His brother Fred's headstone is blank — my cousins haven't decided on what should be written there. His mother's is a simple REST IN PEACE, and on his father's are the lines from Prospero's speech in *The Tempest*: "Our revels now are ended . . ."

I look down at the snowy earth where my father lies. There are footprints under the maple tree that grows over his grave. People have been here, although the snow around the other graves is untrammeled. It was June when we buried him — the summer solstice. The day I return is Ash Wednesday. He lies there in the cold winter ground. I make a snowball with my hands, pack it firm, and lob it gently at the grave. There doesn't seem to be anything else to do here.

Twenty-five

IN THE TOP DRAWERS of my grandmother's desk at Tree-tops, behind the decks of playing cards and balls of saved string, I found some old snapshots of my parents. In the pictures, they are sitting on the lawn in front of one of the houses, and there are some small hemlock bushes behind them — bushes that are knotted, full-grown trees now and block the view of the lake. My parents are young, slender, and tanned, my father in chinos with the legs rolled up and my mother in sneakers and shorts with her hands clasped around her knees. In another picture, we are all in front of the big sliding doors to the garage, with my grandfather's Buick roadster parked in the interior shadows. My parents are holding my infant brother Ben. My mother has long hair and wears a straw hat; my father is lean with sharp features and a hungry, forward tilt to his posture. I sit cross-legged, Indian-style, on the ground, wearing a child's striped T-shirt. My hair has been cut by Hoopie the cook, who snipped away at the edge of a bowl she put on my head like a hat.

❊   ❊   ❊

Everything seemed very calm in the weeks after my father was buried. My brother Fred and his wife flew back to California. A lot of letters came to me and to my mother from people who had known or cared about my father, but aside from reading and answering them there wasn't much to be done. So at the beginning of July my husband and the baby and I went up to Treetops, and later my mother joined us there. The weather was brilliant and clear. The familiarity of the meadows and the gleaming white birches and the golden light on the ferns was comforting, soothing. My father had been to Treetops and loved it passionately, but he had not been there recently, and this gave memories of him there a sepia-tinted, nostalgic glow. The gardens at Treetops are overgrown now, wild honeysuckle has taken over my grandmother's cutting garden, the tennis court is just a flat part of the woods, and the roofs of the greenhouses are shattered. The ornamental lily pond below the Stone House is now an oblong patch of rocks and juniper bush. Treetops itself is a beautiful and sad memory of the past, of a kind of life that people don't live anymore, and of those people, who are now all dead.

One day I took the baby, Sarah, down to the lake for a swim. She splashed and shrieked with pleasure. Our neighbor Ann Blake had lost her husband Roswell during the winter, and when she saw me on the beach she walked over and we sat together on our dock in front of the boathouse.

"I'm sorry to hear about Roswell," I said. I remembered a friendly, broad-shouldered man who had worked at a local camp and helped around the McCorts' place further up the hill.

"Oh, yes, and I'm sorry to hear about John. Who would have thought, last summer? . . ."

We sat together for a moment on the splintery surface of the dock and looked out at the sun glinting on the translucent green water. Our beach is a rocky stretch dotted with weed patches and driftwood. The Blakes' beach next to it is immaculate and sandy. I thought of the hours I had watched as Roswell cleared it, stone by stone, bush by bush. In the distance, the granite peak of Cardigan Mountain dominates the circle of smaller hills around the lake. My father took me up Cardigan when I was five. At the bottom, on the way down, we met two fellow climbers proudly pointing its height out to their admiring wives. When they saw me come out of the woods, one of the wives giggled, and my father winked at her and I knew that he was very proud.

"With Roswell it was sudden," Ann said. "It was in the morning and he fixed my breakfast and I was washing the dishes and he said why don't you come out and I said I'll come out when I'm finished. So I went out and I didn't see him anywhere and I walked around the tractor and there he was, so I ran into the house. You know I had the ambulance number posted right up on the wall, but do you think I could read it? Later they said he was probably gone when I found him, and I thought maybe if I had gone out sooner he would have told me he felt badly and I could have done something, but they said no, it was a massive coronary and he probably wouldn't have had time to say a word to me. I'm just thankful he wasn't up on the hill somewhere, where I wouldn't have known, but now I hear all these noises at night. People ask me how I'm doing and I say fine, fine, I have no choice."

"Well, I think Ann is fine," my mother said later. "But she burst into tears when she saw me." My mother was standing in front of the fireplace in the Stone House.

"Did she tell you about it?"

"She said he was out there . . ."

"I know, she was just finishing the dishes."

"She didn't finish them, she said."

"She's changing her story," I said. "She told me she finished them."

"The point is, how long was he out there?"

"She's changing it. She said to me, if she had gone out there sooner maybe he would have said something and . . ."

"I know how she feels," my mother said. "I tell people I was just going up to get the mail, and it's true, but on the way back I stopped for a look at the flower beds and the lawn . . ."

"But Daddy didn't die!"

"He tried to get up, he broke his leg while I was out there."

"It doesn't matter, he didn't die from a broken leg." When she got back to the house, my father had fallen. The leg was swollen and he groaned in pain. She had to call a neighbor to help lift him back onto the bed. After that, he didn't eat anymore and he slipped quickly away.

"You couldn't watch him every minute, Mary," my husband said.

"I know, but it was awful." I hadn't seen my mother cry, but now she had tears in her eyes and we stopped talking.

At night I am haunted by images. My father's hobbledehoy walk back and forth to the bathroom before he broke his leg. (He wouldn't let anyone help him up, but once he was out of bed there would be a moment when he would stop and waver and you would just go help him without saying anything about it.) My mother in the spring afternoon stopping for a few moments in her flower garden, pulling a weed out of the iris border, a dead blossom off the delphinium stalks. My father getting up and there being no one's help for him to refuse and then no one to help him. My father falling.

Walking down the hill after dinner at Treetops, I hold

the sleeping baby in my arms and look up at the stars. My father taught me their patterns. We studied the constellations on icy nights, standing and walking over the great lawns at Beechwood. We had books and a chart and a cheap telescope. Now I can pick out the W shape of Queen Cassiopeia, and the Big Dipper with the Little Dipper pouring into it, and the disjointed forms of Ursa Major, and the tiny perfect box of Job's Coffin. I wonder if my father is up there somewhere, looking down at us. Has he just vanished into the atmosphere of some fragrant summer night? I ask my husband what he thinks happens after a person dies.

"I guess I believe in reincarnation," he says.

"You think your soul is going to another body? You think another soul is you?"

"Maybe I just don't want to think about it," my husband says. He is fifty-six.

"How can you not think about it?"

"I just don't." He shrugs his shoulders as if to unload the weight of my questions. In the next room the baby cries and he gets up to comfort her.

Later in the summer we are all having dinner at the house in Ossining. My brother is there with his wife, and I am there with my husband and the baby. Everyone says they are fine. There is not much talk about my father. Before we leave, after dinner, the baby starts to cry. It's a summer twilight, and the soft evening light in the downstairs room is as gentle as loss. My mother picks up the baby and half-walks, half-dances her around the room. She reaches the end of the room, near the sideboard where my father always kept his wallet and his reading glasses. There was always a stack of letters from him stamped and waiting to be mailed there. Now I notice that my mother is singing softly to the baby as she circles around back toward the fireplace.

"Bonnie Charlie's gone away," she is singing in a quiet lilting voice, as if she and the baby were far away from us in their own twilit world.

"Oh my heart will break in two," she sings. It's a sad sweet ballad that she used to sing to me so long ago, and she dances in circles next to the sideboard. The baby is quiet now and the rest of us are talking at the table, but I hear my mother singing over the babble of our voices.

"Will he ne'er come back again?" she sings very softly, "will he ne'er come back again?" The baby looks silently over her shoulder. Outside, the darkness drops down over the driveway and the orchard and the vegetable garden where my father spaded the earth and planted lettuce and broccoli, and over the flower beds and the lawns where he won't be walking anymore, and over the porch and the metal chair where he used to sit and read and drink a glass of iced tea, or, before that, gin.

"Will he ne'er come back again?" my mother sings, almost whispering, "will he ne'er come back again?" My eyes fill with tears and our conversation stops, and no one says anything as my mother twirls and sings in the corner of the room and night falls.

ABOUT THE AUTHOR

Susan Cheever was born in New York City in 1943
and is a graduate of Brown University.
She is the author of three novels,
Looking for Work, *A Handsome Man*, and *The Cage*.
At present she lives in New York with her husband,
Calvin Tomkins, and their daughter, Sarah.